Managing Information

For continual improvement

David A. Wilson

*Published in association with
the Institute of Management*

the Institute
of Management

FOUNDATION

BUTTERWORTH
HEINEMANN

.i-Heinemann Ltd
House, Jordan Hill, Oxford OX2 8DP

& A member of the Reed Elsevier group

OXFORD LONDON BOSTON
MUNICH NEW DELHI SINGAPORE SYDNEY
TOKYO TORONTO WELLINGTON

First published 1993
Reprinted 1993

British Library Cataloguing in Publication Data
Wilson, David A.
   Managing Information: for continual improvement
   I. Title
   658.4

ISBN 0 7506 0667 3

Composition by Genesis Typesetting, Laser Quay, Rochester, Kent
Printed and bound in Great Britain by Clays Ltd, St Ives plc

Contents

Series adviser's preface

This book is one of a series designed for people wanting to develop their capabilities as managers. You might think that there isn't anything very new in that. In one way you would be right. The fact that very many people want to learn to become better managers is not new, and for many years a wide range of approaches to such learning and development has been available. These have included courses leading to formal qualifications, organizationally-based management development programmes and a whole variety of self-study materials. A copious literature, extending from academic textbooks to sometimes idiosyncratic prescriptions from successful managers and consultants, has existed to aid – or perhaps confuse – the potential seeker after managerial truth and enlightenment.

So what is new about this series? In fact, a great deal – marking in some ways a revolution in our thinking both about the art of managing and also the process of developing managers.

Where did it all begin? Like most revolutions, although there may be a single, identifiable act that precipitated the uprising, the roots of discontent are many and long-established. The debate about the performance of British managers, the way managers are educated and trained, and the extent to which shortcomings in both these areas have contributed to our economic decline, has been running for several decades.

Until recently, this debate had been marked by periods of frenetic activity – stimulated by some report or enquiry and perhaps ending in some new initiatives or policy changes – followed by relatively long periods of comparative calm. But the underlying causes for concern persisted. Basically, the majority of managers in the UK appeared to have little or no training for their role, certainly far less than their counterparts in our major competitor nations. And there was concern about the nature, style and appropriateness of the management education and training that was available.

The catalyst for this latest revolution came in late 1986 and early 1987, when three major reports reopened the whole issue. The 1987 reports were *The Making of British Managers* by John Constable and Roger McCormick, carried out for the British Institute of Management and the CBI, and *The Making of Managers* by Charles Handy, carried out for the (then) Manpower Services Commission, National Economic Development Office and British Institute of Management. The 1986 report, which often receives less recognition than it deserves as a key contribution to the recent changes, was *Management Training: context and process* by Iain Mangham and Mick Silver, carried out for the

Economic and Social Research Council and the Department of Trade and Industry.

It is not the place to review in detail what the reports said. Indeed, they and their consequences are discussed in several places in this series of books. But essentially they confirmed that:

- British managers were undertrained by comparison with their counterparts internationally.
- The majority of employers invested far too little in training and developing their managers.
- Many employers found it difficult to specify with any degree of detail just what it was that they required successful managers to be able to do.

The Constable/McCormick and Handy reports advanced various recommendations for addressing these problems, involving an expansion of management education and development, a reformed structure of qualifications and a commitment from employers to a code of practice for management development. While this analysis was not new, and had echoes of much that had been said in earlier debates, this time a few leading individuals determined that the response should be both radical and permanent. The response was coordinated by the newly-established Council for Management Education and Development (now the National Forum for Management Education and Development (NFMED)) under the energetic and visionary leadership of Bob (now Sir Bob) Reid of Shell UK (now chairman of the British Railways Board).

Under the umbrella of NFMED a series of employer-led working parties tackled the problem of defining what it was that managers should be able to do, and how this differed for people at different levels in their organizations; how this satisfactory ability to perform might be verified; and how an appropriate structure of management qualifications could be put in place. This work drew upon the methods used to specify vocational standards in industry and commerce, and led to the development and introduction of competence-based management standards and qualifications. In this context, competence is defined as the ability to perform the activities within an occupation or function to the standards expected in employment.

It is this competence-based approach that is new in our thinking about the manager's capabilities. It is also what is new about this series of books, in that they are designed to support both this new structure of management standards, and of development activities based on it. The series was originally commissioned to support the Institute of Management's Certificate and Diploma qualifications, which were one of the first to be based on the new standards. However, these books are equally appropriate to any university, college or indeed company course leading to a certificate in management or diploma in management studies.

The standards were specified through an extensive process of consultation with a large number of managers in organizations of many different types and sizes. They are therefore employment based and employer-supported. And they fill the gap that Mangham and Silver identified – now we do have a language to describe what it is employers want their managers to be able to do – at least in part.

If you are engaged in any form of management development leading to a certificate or diploma qualification conforming to the national management standards, then you are probably already familiar with most of the key ideas on which the standards are based. To achieve their key purpose, which is defined as achieving the organization's objectives and continuously improving its performance, managers need to perform four key roles: managing operations, managing finance, managing people and managing information. Each of these key roles has a sub-structure of units and elements, each with associated performance and assessment criteria.

The reason for the qualification 'in part' is that organizations are different, and jobs within them are different. Thus the generic management standards probably do not cover all the management competences that you may need to possess in your job. There are almost certainly additional things, specific to your own situation in your own organization, that you need to be able to do. The standards are necessary, but almost certainly not sufficient. Only you, in discussion with your boss, will be able to decide what other capabilities you need to possess. But the standards are a place to start, a basis on which to build. Once you have demonstrated your proficiency against the standards, it will stand you in good stead as you progress through your organization, or change jobs.

So how do the new standards change the process by which you develop yourself as a manager? They change the process of development, or of gaining a management qualification, quite a lot. It is no longer a question of acquiring information and facts, perhaps by being 'taught' in some classroom environment, and then being tested to see what you can recall. It involves demonstrating, in a quite specific way, that you can do certain things to a particular standard of performance. And because of this, it puts a much greater onus on you to manage your own development, to decide how you can demonstrate any particular competence, what evidence you need to present, and how you can collect it. Of course, there will always be people to advise and guide you in this, if you need help.

But there is another dimension, and it is to this that this series of books is addressed. While the standards stress ability to perform, they do not ignore the traditional knowledge base that has been associated with 'management studies'. Rather, they set this in a different context. The standards are supported by 'underpinning knowledge and understanding' which has three components:

- Purpose and context, which is knowledge and understanding of the manager's objectives, and of the relevant organizational and environmental influences, opportunities and values.
- Principles and methods, which is knowledge and understanding of the theories, models, principles, methods and techniques that provide the basis of competent managerial performance.
- Data, which is knowledge and understanding of specific facts likely to be important to meeting the standards.

Possession of the relevant knowledge and understanding underpinning the standards is needed to support competent managerial performance as specified in the standards. It also has an important role in supporting the transferability of management capabilities. It helps to ensure that you have done more than learned 'the way we do things around here' in your own organization. It indicates a recognition of the wider things which underpin competence, and that you will be able to change jobs or organizations and still be able to perform effectively.

These books cover the knowledge and understanding underpinning the management standards, most specifically in the category of principles and methods. But their coverage is not limited to the minimum required by the standards, and extends in both depth and breadth in many areas. The authors have tried to approach these underlying principles and methods in a practical way. They use many short cases and examples which we hope will demonstrate how, in practice, the principles and methods, and knowledge of purpose and context plus data, support the ability to perform as required by the management standards. In particular we hope that this type of presentation will enable you to identify and learn from similar examples in your own managerial work.

You will already have noticed that one consequence of this new focus on the standards is that the traditional 'functional' packages of knowledge and theory do not appear. The standard textbook titles such as 'quantitative methods', 'production management', 'organizational behaviour' etc. disappear. Instead, principles and methods have been collected together in clusters that more closely match the key roles within the standards. You will also find a small degree of overlap in some of the volumes, because some principles and methods support several of the individual units within the standards. We hope you will find this useful reinforcement.

Having described the positive aspects of standards-based management development, it would be wrong to finish without a few cautionary remarks. The developments described above may seem simple, logical and uncontroversial. It did not always seem that way in the years of work which led up to the introduction of the standards. To revert to the revolution analogy, the process has been marked by ideological conflict and battles over sovereignty and territory. It has sometimes been unclear which side various parties are on – and indeed how many sides there are! The revolution, if well advanced, is not at an end. Guerrilla warfare continues in parts of the territory.

Perhaps the best way of describing this is to say that, while competence-based standards are widely recognized as at least a major part of the answer to improving managerial performance, they are not the whole answer. There is still some debate about the way competences are defined, and whether those in the standards are the most appropriate on which to base assessment of managerial performance. There are other models of management competences than those in the standards.

There is also a danger in separating management performance into a set of discrete components. The whole is, and needs to be, more than the sum of the parts. Just like bowling an off-break in cricket, practising a golf swing or forehand drive in tennis, you have to combine all the separate movements into a smooth, flowing action. How you combine the competences, and build on them, will mark your own individual style as a manager.

We should also be careful not to see the standards as set in stone. They determine what today's managers need to be able to do. As the arena in which managers operate changes, then so will the standards. The lesson for all of us as managers is that we need to go on learning and developing, acquiring new skills or refining existing ones. Obtaining your certificate or diploma is like passing a mile post, not crossing the finishing line.

All the changes and developments of recent years have brought management qualifications, and the processes by which they are gained, much closer to your job as a manager. We hope these books support this process by providing bridges between your own experience and the underlying principles and methods which will help you to demonstrate your competence. Already, there is a lot of evidence that managers enjoy the challenge of demonstrating competence, and find immediate benefits in their jobs from the programmes based on these new-style qualifications. We hope you do too. Good luck in your career development.

Paul Jervis

Preface

If you are a manager somewhere in the middle of your organization, you had better hold tight: the changes you have had to adjust to recently are only the beginning. We are in the middle of a revolution right now – the information revolution – which is having a greater effect on work and employment than the industrial revolution ever had. And this time the changes are being compressed into a much shorter period.

As the changes come along thicker and faster, you are expected to deal with the crises they cause at work. But for how long can you survive? If you think there must be a better way than just reacting to each new situation, then you are right, there is. But it requires you to take a little time out each day from the urgent problems to consider the important problems. It may be urgent that you meet that deadline today, but it is far more important that you make progress towards that better way, because if you don't, you and your organization will soon have no deadlines left to meet.

I would advise you to make yourself as valuable as possible to your (or any other) organization, because your job is under threat from the computer. White collar middle managers are losing their jobs, and when it happens they are bewildered. Why has it happened? Why me? – they ask. The writing was on the wall but they could not see it; the computer is dispossessing them of their jobs in the same way the combine harvester dispossessed farm labourers of theirs – except for the few who understood machinery and could keep it running.

So, make sure you can read the writing on the wall, and prepare yourself. Start thinking about how else you could manage information at work, not just to save costs, but to offer a better deal to your customers. And start thinking about demonstrating your competence to your boss by working towards the new competence-based Certificate in Management being promoted by the Management Charter Initiative. This book is written to help you get started.

David A. Wilson

1 The difference information can make

Why is this chapter relevant?

The rate of change in the business world during the 1980s was fast, and during the 1990s we can already see that change is occurring faster and it is likely to get even faster still. To survive in this environment, organizations must learn to be flexible and responsive to their customers' needs.

You will have to help the organization you work for become more flexible and responsive, or you may find one day soon that you no longer have an organization to work for.

This introductory chapter sets the scene – describes the changing business environment – and shows that information and the way it is managed are the keys to survival and success.

> Frowning, John swung round from his desk, walked across his office to the percolator and poured a cup of black coffee. Through the huge window he could see clouds building beyond the Assembly Shop. There were no lights on outside. The assembly workers had gone home three hours ago and the plant was quiet.
>
> The aroma from his cup reminded him of holidays with Ann and the kids . . . breakfast in the sunshine with French bread, cherry jam and steaming hot coffee. That seemed so long ago, and now here he was again, wrestling with cashflows and profit forecasts, with no obvious escape from the relentless squeeze between low revenue and rising costs. He looked across at the spreadsheet glowing brightly on the screen of his personal computer. 'The trouble is' he thought, 'we've already made all the obvious cuts. All that's left are fixed costs, and if we cut those, we cut our revenue.' On impulse he strode across to the keyboard, increased sales prices by 25 per cent and watched the new figures cascade through to a healthy balance on the bottom line. Gloomily he knew the market wouldn't bear price rises of 25 per cent. 'I'm not playing "what-if" here,' he thought to himself, 'I'm playing "if-only".'

Recognize the scenario? Perhaps you do because helping to run a successful organization is difficult – and rapidly getting more difficult as markets become more competitive and consumers become more demanding.

However, there is a way out through 'better management' – which in other books might be tackled under the headings of marketing, finance or operations, but here will be explained in terms of how you and others in your organization manage information.

In the opening scenario, John is wrestling with poor margins coupled with inelasticity of demand – a typical problem in today's competitive markets – and yet in many markets there are players who can apparently charge a premium for their services or products. Furthermore, the basic service or product offered by these privileged players is often not very different from that offered by less successful players in the same market: the premium product often clearly requires similar inputs of direct labour and direct materials. So how is it they can charge more? It must be the way the direct labour and materials are put together. Now here's the key: the way they are put together depends upon that magic ingredient – information – whose cost per sale is often a fixed cost which halves every time you double your output.

The value of information

When you want a sandwich for lunch, do you buy the cheap, dried up one from the crumby tray – or given the chance would you select a more expensive creation which is carefully packed and looks fresh and appetizing? You would probably choose the more expensive sandwich, unless you are down to your last dime – or at any rate more and more consumers would, as expectations and disposable income gradually increase.

Quality and design are clearly very important factors in determining the price which the consumer will pay for products or services. It is true for trivial items such as sandwiches and it is also true for major purchases such as cars. Compare the two specifications for 5-speed 5-seat 1300cc saloons shown in Figure 1.1.

On the face of it these two cars are very similar, and yet the slightly smaller, less powerful of the two is just twice the price of the other. Even so, you will probably not be surprised to learn that in the UK the

Model	Power (bhp)	Length (in)	Width (in)	Height (in)	Weight (cwt)	Max Spd (mph)	Accel. 0–60 (s)	Fuel cons. (mpg)	Price (£)
VW Polo 1.3CL	55	159	63	53	15.6	95	14.5	41.7	8070
Lada Riva 1300L	72	162	64	56	20.8	90	15.9	31.4	3999

Figure 1.1   *Specifications and prices of Lada Riva and VW Polo*

modern design, better quality VW outsells the bigger, more powerful Lada.

So what can we learn from this example? The main lesson is that from the customer's point of view the VW represents a far more attractive combination of raw materials than the Lada. In other words, starting with the same kinds of input – similar materials and probably similar amounts of direct labour – one manufacturer builds in more know-how and thereby adds more value than the other. Know-how of course includes, for example, design information, quality information and production information. Presumably the manufacturers of the Lada would like to know how to build a better car and charge more for it and thus it seems their problem is directly related to how they manage information.

How to manage information

All organizations must manage information, just as all businesses must make a profit, but for a chief executive to tell you to improve your information management, like telling you to improve profits, is no help at all. What you need is more specific direction on the route to those overall goals, and that is what this book aims to do.

But before we rush on too far, is it fair to elevate managing information to the same level of importance as making a profit? It could be argued that however well you manage information, without profits your business will fail. On the other hand, without information decisions are impossible, and profitability depends upon good decision making throughout the organization. Decision-making is central to every manager's role, and whole books have been devoted to just this subject by authors such as Herbert Simon and Peter Drucker who belong to, and have helped create, the decision-making school of management thought, the importance of which is difficult to overestimate.

Decisions are impossible without information and managers are constantly seeking more and better information to support their decision making, hence the growth of information systems – a term which today is often taken to mean networks of computers, but strictly speaking should also include non-computerized channels of communication such as regular meetings, the in- and out-trays full of memos and reports and of course the phone. To survive, every organization must have an information system. All organizations must be able to collect information, communicate it internally and process it so that managers can make decisions quickly and effectively in pursuit of organizational objectives in a changing, competitive environment. The information system is the nervous system which allows an organization to respond to opportunities and avoid threats; to be effective it must reach into the furthest extremities of the organization.

The role of computers

Computers and electronic communications networks are destined to play an ever bigger role in the handling of information for three reasons. First, computers can be so much cheaper for storing and distributing information than the old paperwork systems with their cumbersome mailing and filing. In some instances computers can generate massive permanent savings by completely removing the need for large amounts of routine paperwork and the army of clerks who process it. An everyday example is the demise of the cheque book. You may have noticed recently that your bank statements show many more automatic entries such as card purchases, direct debits and automated cash, and rather fewer cheque entries. Not long ago thousands of millions of cheques where drawn annually in the UK. Each cheque had to be physically transported to the recipient's bank for cashing, then returned to its home bank for deducting from the drawer's account. Machines were used for sorting and processing, but only after each individual cheque had been manually encoded by banking personnel using a keyboard device called a magnetic character inscriber. The banks used to spend literally millions of man- and woman-hours on clearing cheques – a strong incentive for them to get rid of this paperwork system and replace it with automatic payments where funds are transferred electronically.

The second reason why networks of computers are becoming widespread is their ability to speed up the whole trading cycle, resulting in more productive use of assets and faster response to customer requirements. For instance the buyers in organizations are beginning to link up their computers with those of their suppliers so they can exchange information electronically. Using electronic data interchange (EDI) the whole process of inviting tenders, receiving quotations, placing orders, receiving the invoices and paying – which used to take weeks using the postal service can now be completed the same day if necessary. EDI offers lots of advantages: the money comes back to the seller more quickly, the buyer needs lower stocks to support a given level of trading, and planning is much easier for both. In fact once installed, EDI makes the whole process easier, making it much more likely that orders will go to suppliers who have EDI links with their customers.

The third reason why computers are sure to take over in more and more areas of organizational life is that they can make any information already collected for one purpose instantly available to be used for many other secondary purposes. This is opening up totally new ways of using information. Let us take for example the way information about groceries bought by customers can be used in a retail outlet. In corner shops the till is often operated by the proprietor and once the customer has paid for his or her purchases the only record of the transactions is on the till roll – to all intents and purposes inaccessible. It is of little consequence though because the proprietor is close enough to the action for decision making and knows roughly what the day's takings were, how many customers have been served, and whether there has been a run on a particular item.

In the supermarket however, there may be thirty checkout operators and 10 000 or more different lines stocked. At peak times items may be leaving the supermarket at a rate of 40 000 items per hour. Stocks of each line must be reordered to arrive at the rate of consumption, or changing demand for particular lines caused by promotional activity or food scares could easily lead to empty shelves or overstocking. The supermarket therefore cannot afford to throw away till roll data collected anyway to work out how much to charge the customer – the primary use. Once collected it must be used again for stock control, a secondary use. And that's not the end of the story: information is expensive to collect, but once held in digital form it costs next to nothing to store and so can be freely used over and over again for a variety of secondary purposes. As a last example, till roll data collected over a period of months or years can be analysed for long-term trends and presented graphically to aid in forecasting and strategic planning.

Information overload

At a personal level we all know that more information of every type is now available than ever before. How often nowadays are you 'personally selected' both at home and at work, for the chance of receiving a fabulous holiday – and some information? Most of it is junk information – junk mail, junk faxes and junk memos which you file straight away in the waste paper bin – and guess who personally selected you? A computer of course. Computers are great for sending out information: more computers are used for word processing than for any other task. They are also amazingly fast at processing some types of data, in particular financial and numerical data once it has been converted into electronic digital signals, but no computer yet invented can receive an item of junk mail, read it and decide what to do with it.

So history is repeating itself: the invention of the typewriter with its high output of thirty or forty words per minute did not lead us to employ fewer scribes to write letters and other documents. Instead we employed more people to produce much more written work and now the word processor is having the same effect. The net result is more people with keyboard skills than ever before, and far more information on every conceivable subject, competing for our attention and, more often than not, failing to get it.

It seems that computers which are used to help us manage information by processing data faster, far from solving our problems are actually creating new problems by adding to the volume, variety and complexity of information available. Nevertheless some organizations thrive in this new environment; they use computers and modern information systems to make better decisions more quickly, allowing them to respond faster to customer requirements, which in markets today is a massive competitive advantage.

Responsiveness to customer needs

Nobody likes being kept waiting, and we are often prepared to pay to avoid it. When you get back from your holidays you can save money by posting off your holiday snaps to a cut-price processor – or you can pay a premium to have them back within the hour from Supasnaps or Boots in the High Street.

Business customers don't like to be kept waiting either; it can actually cost them money, and so suppliers who deliver promptly have a significant edge on their competitors. To be able to deliver standard items fast, suppliers need only hold stocks, but for products designed specially to the customer's requirements, stock holding is not possible. The ability to deliver promptly then depends upon how well the organization can marshall its resources to make and deliver to meet the customer's order. And that involves fast, efficient handling of information – about what to make and how to make it.

One company that understands this is Yamasaki Mazak, a Japanese machine-tool manufacturer whose factory is in Worcester, close to Coventry where British manufacturers once made and supplied machine tools around the world. Mazak operate an automated factory that carries few stocks of finished goods and yet can deliver to their customers' specifications within one or two months. This is amazingly fast when you consider that other manufacturers typically quote a six month delivery. Mazak never make batches of product, as used to be the custom in Coventry. In this way they keep each of the stages in the manufacturing process free of the logjams and queues which develop with batch production. Thus they can speed their customers' special requirements through the factory without delay. The Mazak factory produces up to 100 machines a month, in a range of fifty-five different models. Each model has optional features and so they seldom produce the same product twice running. Each order requires a different set of manufacturing instructions.

The only way they can do this is by making extensive use of CAD (computer-aided design), CAM (computer-aided manufacture) and CIM (computer-integrated manufacture). Customer orders and specifications are processed on the screens of CAD workstations. Then this design information is transferred electronically to the screen of process planners who work at CAM workstations. Here the design information is converted into CNC (computer numerical control) programs which are used to control the automatic machine-tool processes used in the factory. A paperwork system just would not be fast enough. All the computers and machine tool processes are linked up together through a computer network, and the whole production process is scheduled and coordinated by a supervisory computer to form an advanced example of CIM.

And what does this all mean to the customer? It means taking delivery of an individually designed, high quality product only two months after placing the order instead of six months – bringing forward the payback period or break-even point by a massive four months. No wonder the Japanese dominate the world market in machine tools. Yamasaki Mazak are truly world-class performers.

World markets

Factories like the Mazak one in Worcester are not a curious phenomenon that we can afford to ignore: they represent the pattern of the future. Our cosy, protected home markets are disappearing fast, as the Americans and Japanese buy companies or build factories here. The distinction between home and export markets is disappearing, as tariffs, quotas and technical barriers to trade across Europe are removed. The world is rapidly becoming a global marketplace in which only the world-class players thrive.

This is great news for us as consumers because it means we can choose from the best value products and services available in the world. But as managers of organizations it means we face dramatically increased competition.

World class performance

World class is a term used by Dick Schonberger, an American consultant and professor at the University of Washington, to describe any organization which is consistently held in the highest regard by its customers, and can therefore compete successfully in world markets. Tom Peters, another American, author of *In Search of Excellence* and *Thriving on Chaos* describes these organizations as excellent. The important point to note however is that somehow, these excellent, world-class organizations are consistently able to meet and often exceed their customers' expectations.

This kind of exceptional performance cannot happen by chance: it must be made to happen by applying a systematic approach with great dedication. Why? Because customer expectations are constantly rising. What we as consumers are delighted to receive today, we come to expect tomorrow, and so any organization that stands still on quality and customer service is soon left behind.

The only way to excel in world markets is through continual improvement. The Japanese word for improvement is kaizen, a word which they now use in a business context to describe the group of techniques used to achieve continual systematic improvement. In the west we group together the same techniques under the title of total quality management, or TQM.

Total Quality Management

The TQM bandwagon is rolling in the UK, promoted actively by the Department of Trade and Industry through its 'Managing into the 90s' initiative. The DTI has been converted to the view that the ability to believe fervently in a better future is not a uniquely Japanese characteristic. British employees – managers and workers together – are also capable of sharing a fervent belief in a better future. Under the right circumstances it can become a self-fulfilling belief, which is not dependent on a kamikaze culture but upon the human characteristics of hope, ambition, intellect and team spirit. The DTI is using TQM as a medium for getting the message across to British organizations: the old styles of management which seemed to work at the beginning of the century, clearly don't work any longer. The old styles of management depended on delegation of authority and responsibility from the brainy top, down to the brawny bottom levels. Organizations in which a few managers manage, and many labourers labour become victims of the intellectual bottleneck at the top. Too many changes are needed on too many fronts for the few at the top to take all the decisions necessary – or even to monitor them all closely. Instead, the new styles of management recognize that workers too are – or at any rate should be – managers to some extent. Indeed the terms 'management' and 'workers' perpetuate outdated attitudes such as the 'ours is not to reason why' attitude at lower levels, and the 'you don't need to know about that' attitude at higher levels. The new successful organizations are those in which managers are coaches rather than sergeant-majors, where information is more freely accessible, and where everyone makes an intellectual contribution to a better future. It all sounds too revolutionary for some chief executives to stomach: it seems to require a supreme act of faith – to abandon the deeply held old beliefs about how managers manage, and to replace them with new radically different methods. But for those chief executives who do take the plunge, the rewards have proved staggering. For instance in 1981 British Airways was losing on average £200 per minute, until CEO Sir Colin Marshall launched 'Putting People First' – a TQM programme. Within three years BA was profitable again, and has remained so even through the Gulf crisis and the recession when other major world airlines were struggling – and some like Pan Am failing – to survive. So what is TQM? Organizations like to customize their TQM programmes and promote them internally under a variety of different names. But in fact 'Putting People First' at BA has much in common with 'kaizen' at the Nissan plant in Sunderland, with 'Market Driven Quality' at the IBM plant at Havant, with 'First Service' at

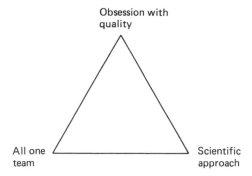

Figure 1.2   *The Joiner triangle*

W H Smiths, and with 'Quality, Efficiency, Service To All' (QUEST) at Oxford County Council.

All these programmes can be thought of as TQM because to some extent, they all address the three essential requirements for continual improvement. These are neatly summarized in the Joiner triangle (Figure 1.2) devised by Brian Joiner, of Joiner Associates, Wisconsin USA, to drive home their fundamental importance. Let us take a brief look at each of these essentials because as we shall see, information management underpins them all.

Obsession with quality

Quality in this context does not have its usual meaning of conformance to specification. Instead, to underline the importance of the customer these days, it is defined as 'exceeding customer expectations'. This dramatic change in thinking comes as a major culture shock to organizations first exposed to TQM, and managing the change to achieve this revolution must start, as we have seen, right at the top, with the chief executive. Without total commitment from the chief executive the lengthy training programmes for spreading the TQM gospel will be just another costly burden on the organization. There are so many instances of chief executives sounding off about the importance of quality, and then compromising as soon as the pressure is on. Managers at every level take their lead from what the chief executive does, and they ignore the rhetoric. Actions speak louder than words, and TQM will only work when the whole organization from top to bottom is truly obsessed with quality in its newly understood sense.

Managing change of this magnitude requires information management of the highest order because of the far-reaching effects of change on the motivation and working practices of everyone in the workforce team.

All one team

The focus on the customer in TQM programmes needs explaining because another new concept is used, that of the 'internal customer'. It is used to emphasize how important it is for individuals and departments to work together as a team, rather than pursuing narrow local objectives and blaming each other or passing the buck when things go wrong. Dick Schonberger talks of building a chain of customers, where the 'customer' is defined as the person or department that receives the output of each person's or department's work, regardless of whether they are inside or outside the organization. When this can be done, the result is a workforce who pull together as a team towards overall objectives, rather than focusing on narrow departmental objectives and pulling the organization apart by competing internally.

Teamwork of course depends on good communications and the free flow of information within the organization. Communications problems are usually more severe in larger organizations, and progressive bigger companies are seeking ways to improve communications. One approach being tried by British Airways, British Petroleum and others, is to adopt new organizational structures with fewer layers in the hierarchy – the so-called flatter organization. Also, many companies are investing in computer networks to provide management information, with a personal computer on every manager's desk. These are two ways of 'enabling' managers throughout the organization, by making it easier for them to get hold of the information they need to do their job, to cooperate, and to pull together as a team.

Scientific approach

Can you imagine playing hunt the thimble without someone calling 'getting warmer' or 'colder'? Progress towards any goal requires change, and quick feedback to indicate whether the most recent change brought you nearer or further from your goal. In fact the more information you have the better: it is useful to know how much nearer or further – and that requires measurement, a theme we shall return to later.

Thus to improve something at work, you must change it in some way. An improvement is simply a change for the better, and the TQM philosophy of continual improvement should encourage everyone constantly to be on the lookout for small changes they can make to improve customer satisfaction. Unfortunately however, organizations for producing goods or services are usually very complex systems, especially if they are of any size. There are thousands upon thousands of factors which can affect customer satisfaction, some of which you can control, and some of which you cannot. You can control what goes on in your own outfit, but not what goes on outside. The perceptions of your customers are influenced by what is on offer elsewhere, the economic climate and so on. These you cannot control, and to make matters worse the influence of these external factors is constantly changing. So the net result is that although you as a manager can easily recognize the need for change, it is seldom clear what you should change – or in what way.

Even when you do make a change, it is sometimes difficult so see whether it is an improvement or not, because there may be a delay before the results feed through, or because when the results do arrive they may be swamped by the effects of external influences. Dr Eli Goldratt, a consultant to General Motors and other multinationals, puts it in a nutshell. 'For improvement you must decide just three things: what to change, to change to what, and how to change.'

In deciding what to change we need to develop a deeper understanding of what is important in our business – the critical success factors. We also need to decide in which direction to change them. In other words we need to understand cause–effect relationships. Dr William Edwards Deming, an American statistician refers to all of this as profound knowledge. He advocates the use of simple statistical methods to isolate the few important influences from among the many less important ones, and to help predict the effect of changes. The Japanese certainly think Deming knows what he is talking about because back in the early 1950s Deming was a lecturer and consultant to hundreds of top Japanese business men, and they still credit much of their subsequent industrial success and economic power to his methods. He has been decorated by the Emperor and honoured by the inauguration of an annual industrial quality award in his name.

To sum up then, what we mean by a scientific approach is no more than a systematic, methodical way of collecting, analysing and interpreting information, using measurements to prove we are on the right track and monitor our progress.

Measurements and numbers

The ultimate measure of success of course is profit, but as we saw earlier, the goal of maximizing profits is not particularly helpful in suggesting how to achieve that goal. To quote Goldratt again, he suggests that the goal should be 'to make more money now and in future.' He concedes however this is only a marginally better guide, and it needs breaking down into more detailed supporting goals. The three he suggests for manufacturers are raising throughput, at the same time as lowering inventory and reducing operating expense. In fact Goldratt has special definitions for throughput, inventory and operating expense, but clearly they are capable of being measured in terms of revenue, volume or expense. These measures can be charted and thus when you make a change to the manufacturing system you can quickly see whether the change has resulted in an improvement.

This is exactly the approach adopted in Japanese factories where huge charts are to be seen everywhere, for monitoring key performance indicators. By this means they are able to secure the continuous improvement of their processes, quickly cancelling any trials which cause the indicators to deteriorate, and thus consolidating and protecting all previous improvement. This is in stark contrast to the crisis management, or fire-fighting styles of management adopted in less methodical organizations, where financial problems or customer complaints result in knee-jerk responses from management who feel they must be seen to be taking decisive action. These ill-considered, short-term management reactions are likely to do as much harm as good in the long run, and in such organizations there can be no steady but continuous improvement in performance.

Collecting and presenting performance figures can be tiresome and repetitive, but computers are ideal for automating much of the task.

Management information systems

In this introductory chapter we have taken a tour through many areas where information is used in organizations. Computers are commonplace at work now but still only a small proportion of a manager's total information needs are supplied by computers. However you must know from your own experience that PCs are so cheap that department managers can buy them out of petty cash almost, and as a result they are popping up like mushrooms wherever there is a need to store or process information. You know the syndrome: your records are getting in a mess and you are on the point of buying some new filing cabinets but can't find floor space for them. A couple of your more reliable staff have been going on for some time about how the records should be held on computer and so you decide to give them their chance. For you to automate on an *ad hoc* departmental basis like this is fine up to a point, because it is an efficient way of solving local problems. However separate managers solving their individual problems like this create 'islands of information', which do nothing for the flow of information and cooperation between departments. More often than not managers end up with many different and incompatible brands of hardware and software which cannot be linked up easily, thus destroying any chance of developing a corporate information strategy. Information in the form of a printout from one computer system must then be passed to the next department where it is immediately re-keyed back into their different computer system. This is an utter nonsense from a corporate point of view. It is labour intensive, time consuming and inaccurate, allowing the inevitable transcription errors to occur, but more seriously the stacks of printouts create bottlenecks in the information flow, making it impossible for the organization to respond quickly to market and customer needs.

What should happen in theory is that someone should take a look at the information requirements of the organization as a whole and then develop an efficient system to meet those requirements. If this is to happen it is often necessary to hire computer consultants who have experience of developing such systems. This so-called top-down planning is not entirely incompatible with the bottom-up implementation that is so common. However, if implementation is allowed to proceed too far before a plan is in place, the existing heavy investment in incompatible sub-systems will pre-empt its execution.

The challenge

Technology and politics are changing the business world. You as a manager need to be aware of these changes. You need to be aware of what is going on and equip yourself with the new skills required by organizations for survival in a rapidly changing environment.

Flexibility and responsiveness are paramount, and these abilities of course depend on information – the way it is collected, processed and acted upon.

In the following chapters we will examine in more detail some of the ways in which information can be managed within organizations to improve flexibility and responsiveness. Some of the topics you may find more immediately relevant than others, but study them all: they will add to your competence as a manager to meet the challenges of the 1990s and beyond.

Competence self-assessment

Here are some questions that may help you to focus in on any weak spots in your portfolio of managerial skills and knowledge.

1   What would you say are the main corporate objectives of your organization? Some, but not all organizations publicize a corporate mission statement which will outline these. Do you know what they are? If so, write them down.

2   List the main types of information that your organization must collect in order to meet its objectives and carry out its functions.

3   Are there any types of information that your organization should be collecting but is not? List three types of information that your organization could collect which may allow it to become more responsive to its 'customers'.

4 Do you suffer from information overload? – or shortage of information? If so, briefly describe in general terms without reference to technology, the nature of your problem.

5 Write five lines under each of the following headings to describe how your problems in question 4 could be overcome:

● The organization
● Information systems
● Other considerations

6 Write down the main changes that have taken place over the last five years to the services or products supplied by your organization. What trends do these indicate, and where could these trends lead to in another five years?

7 Write down three initiatives you should personally take, to prepare yourself for the changes you think likely in the next five years.

8 Write down three initiatives you think your organization should take, to prepare itself for the changes you think likely in the next five years.

9 Write five lines under each of the following headings to describe how each could benefit through better information management:

● Teamwork
● Quality
● Efficiency
● Effectiveness

10 The total system for collecting and distributing information throughout your organization may or may not make use of computers and digital information. Suggest one local improvement, not necessarily involving computers, which you can cost-justify.

References and further reading

What Car? (1991). Buyers guide – new car prices and specifications. *What Car?*, August, Haymarket Motoring Magazines.

Management Today (1991). Britain's best factories. *Management Today*, May, Management Publications Ltd.

Schonberger, R. J. (1986). *World Class Manufacturing: The Lessons of Simplicity Applied*. The Free Press, Macmillan Inc.

Schonberger, R. J. (1990). *Building a Chain of Customers*. Hutchinson.

Peters, T. (1987). *Thriving on Chaos. Handbook for a Management Revolution.* Macmillan, London.

Department of Trade and Industry. *The route ahead – a directory of publications and videos available under the Managing into the '90s programme.* Department of Trade and Industry.

Department of Trade and Industry. *The quality gurus – what can they do for your company?* Managing into the '90s. Department of Trade and Industry.

Goldratt, E. M. and Cox, J. (1984). *The Goal: Excellence in Manufacturing.* North River Press

Deming, W. E. (1988). *Out of the Crisis.* Cambridge University Press.

Note: Both the above DTI publications can be obtained free of charge by contacting: DTI, c/o Mediascene Ltd, PO Box 90, Hengoed, Mid Glamorgan, CF8 9YE. Telephone: (0443) 821877, Fax: (0443) 822055.

2 How organizations handle information

Why is this chapter relevant?

It is important for you as a manager to appreciate the information needs of your colleagues as well as your own. This chapter deals with concepts and principles, and later gives practical examples of operational information and some common ways of handling it.

The way organizations handle information is important because it affects just about everything they do. For instance, bureaucratic organizations are formal, slow and ponderous in the way they handle information, whereas new, small organizations with everyone working in the same room perhaps, tend to be less formal, fast and flexible.

Specialists who study the way organizations handle information used to be called O & M analysts and they spent most of their time designing pro-forma forms, reports and other paperwork. Their modern equivalents are known as systems analysts and designers. They also spend most of their time thinking about how best to handle information, but that now often means getting rid of paperwork. We will take a closer look at systems in Chapter 5.

Information types and channels

Is information a corporate resource, in some ways similar to other resources such as capital equipment, raw materials, or finance? The courts seem to think so for certain types of information, such as product designs, best-sellers and computer programs, which they refer to as intellectual property. This kind of information has required effort and expense to produce, and it has value because copies of it can be sold. The courts recognize the rights of ownership of this kind of property and are prepared to protect it.

But information is different when compared to finance or capital equipment, because a particular machine can only manifest itself once, and copies are almost as difficult to make as the original, whereas a software program or a novel can be reproduced easily, millions of times if necessary.

We can categorize information according to its market value. Broadly there are three types of information:

- Information for sale, such as software which can be used, or news which informs, or a video or novel which entertains. This is usually privately owned, and access to it is sold by the owner at the market price. Often it has a limited shelf-life, its value declining with time.

- Information given freely, such as train and passenger jet timetables, which has been made available by the owners, because it is in their interests to do so. Advertisements and promotional material fall into this category. Although the information itself is freely available, third parties such as publishers and database operators can often charge for access to such information.
- Information for internal use by organizations, which is never intended to be sold, and is only of legitimate value to the user, such as production schedules, sales forecasts, budgets and minutes of meetings.

All organizations use these types of information. Organizations cannot function for long without it. It is their lifeblood, essential for decision-making and control. It allows them to anticipate changes in an increasingly changeable business environment and to respond effectively to their clients and customers. Information on actual performance must be compared with planned performance, and in the event of a difference, appropriate action must be decided upon. Also to maintain efficiency, information on outputs must be compared with information on inputs, so that appropriate action can be taken to improve the ratio.

As you might realize, it is the information for internal use which we are most concerned with in this book, and the value of such information is always difficult to establish, because there is no external market for it. We do know that its value depends upon factors such as its:

- relevance
- completeness
- accuracy
- clarity
- timeliness

– because these factors affect its usefulness in decision-making, and have a direct bearing on the organization's ability to respond to market needs. Today the consumer is king. That is truer now than it has ever been before.

For a time, just after the Second World War, the British public gratefully accepted whatever our own home-grown private and public sectors provided. At that time there were few imported goods and virtually no competition as manufacturers concentrated on volume at the expense of quality and prompt delivery, in their attempts to keep up with demand. And the public sector, largely protected from competition by state-granted monopolies, grew bureaucratic and unresponsive to an uncomplaining market. The poor consumer had only one choice – take it or leave it – and that applied both to goods and services.

But now taxpayers expect a better deal; the public and service sectors are monitored by watchdogs such as Oftel, audited by bodies such as the Audit Commission, and exposed to competition from the private sector through privatization and compulsory competitive tendering.

The net result is that all organizations are being forced to be more responsive to the needs of the consumer, who is being offered a bewildering range of alternatives by competing organizations, and will walk away – withdrawing financial support – from organizations that fail to meet their needs.

All organizations have routines for collecting and disseminating information. They may consist of simple pro-formas or logs filled out by hand at the end of each day, they may be highly automated data collection systems using the latest technology, or most often, they are something in between these extremes, combining manual and computerized, formal and informal routines.

Information can be communicated in many ways. Here are a few examples:

- Telephone – for quick, informal one-to-one communications.
- Meetings – for more formal discussions.
- Written material – for less immediate, more permanent messages, eg memos, reports, house journals, etc.
- Computer networks – for e-mail.
- Computer disks – for transferring data, also for training material.
- Videos – for training.
- Audio tapes – for training, also for note taking.

Information to aid decision-making

Managers make their decisions in support of the objectives of their organization. But the types of decision taken – and the information

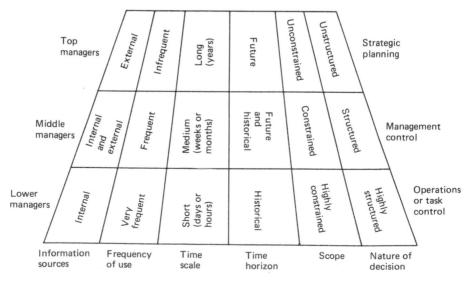

Figure 2.1 *Top managers plan; lower manager control*

	Top managers (Strategic planning)	Middle managers (Management control)	Lower managers (Operations/Task control)
Job title	Operations director	Factory manager	Production manager
Typical decision	Planning new factories and new products	To find the best way to make new products. To budget for existing products	To work to sales targets. To achieve production targets
Information sources	External: sites, markets, economic and social trends	External: raw materials, new machines and labour. Internal: stocks and production	Internal: orders outstanding, resource availability and deployment
Frequency of decision	Infrequent and irregular	Every quarter, or every month perhaps for budgets	By the hour, or daily
Time scale	New factories, new products take a year or more to come on stream	Budgets are quarterly. New production lines take months to install	Production supervised hourly, monitored daily
Time horizon	Forward looking to steer the organization	Future planning and historical monitoring	Mostly historical, comparing achieved output against targets
Scope	Unsconstrained. Searching for the right questions as well as the right answers. What else could or should be planned instead of new factory?	Constrained to meet the plans of top managers	Highly constrained, to meet budgets, targets, forecasts
Nature of decision	Unstructured. Often no clear precedents to follow in decision making.	Semi-structured. Many decisions and plans have precedents and methodology, e.g. network analysis, budgeting etc.	Highly structured. Well developed routines and procedures for production and operations management

Figure 2.2 *The decisions managers make*

needs – are different at different levels in the organization. According to R. N. Anthony of Harvard:

- Senior managers must carry out the strategic planning. They must develop overall goals and methods of achieving them.
- Middle managers have the job of management control. They must ensure these overall goals are achieved effectively and efficiently.

- Junior managers are responsible for task or operational control. They must ensure specific tasks are carried out effectively and efficiently.

The overall picture is that while top managers do more planning, middle and lower managers spend more time controlling to those plans. Of course all managers do some planning and some controlling: it is the proportions that vary at different levels in the organization. The whole picture is summarized in Figure 2.1.

This may seem too theoretical, so let's take an example of a large manufacturing organization which has headquarters staff, and several factories. If we were to look at three managers at senior, middle and junior levels and the decisions they have to take, we might find the pattern to be like that shown in Figure 2.2

I think it is worth pointing out however that R. N. Anthony's analysis described above, assumes a fairly bureaucratic organizational model, based mainly upon larger American organizations in the 1960s and 1970s. There is now a new breed of management writers who are saying that the old bureaucracies are no longer competitive in world markets. Tom Peters, already mentioned in Chapter 1, and James Belasco reckon the new business environment of faster change and greater competition requires 'flatter' organization structures with only a skeleton headquarters staff, much less centralized control, and empowerment of people throughout the organization to change things for the better.

This new style of management will of course require information to be handled more freely and openly. It will affect the design of systems for handling information.

Information for competitive edge

Quality, flexibility and responsiveness. These are the strategic issues of today. Organizations that don't understand this new discipline are declining and will eventually disappear, as other more flexible organizations take over their role by offering better perceived value. It has already happened to much of the UK manufacturing industry as a result of increased competition from Japan and other countries during the 1970s and 1980s. Japan in particular understands the vital importance of quality and flexibility, and they are now moving into our service sectors too. For instance in the London financial markets, Japanese banks already own more banking assets in the City than do the UK banks.

To succeed in the new era of global competition, organizations need relevant, timely and accurate information on:

- Market research, to be responsive.
- Quality control, to produce high quality.

- Progress, to deliver on time.
- Budgets and costs, to offer good value.
- Design, to offer variety.
- Sales, to match demand.

An information system is needed to coordinate and control the flow of information in an organization, like the nervous system of an animal. Paperwork systems used to be satisfactory, but like the dinosaurs are becoming extinct because they are too cumbersome to survive in today's world markets. For organizations of any size, a computer network is now virtually essential.

Also, the shape of the information system must reflect the chains of command and channels of communication shown on the organization chart. As we will see later in Chapter 5, the architecture of the information system must be suited to the organizational structure. An information system which is designed for R. N. Anthony's type of organization is unlikely to serve well the needs of the flatter, more flexible organizations necessary for survival in today's world markets.

Information for teamwork

Tom Peters attacks the classical organization structure for encouraging people to protect their 'turf' – by which he means their function or department. The old style organization encourages company politics, internal competition between departments and buck-passing. Organizations that behave like this are wasting energy: if they pull themselves apart like this with internal conflicts and tensions, they are unlikely to perform well in competition with other organizations where the members are pulling together as a team.

Peters is not the only one trying to get departments within organizations to work together in a spirit of cooperation rather than conflict. Richard Schonberger suggests that companies should build a 'chain of customers' right through the organization, where each person or department regards any other person or department receiving their work output, as a customer whether inside or outside the organization. The concept of the internal customer has been widely accepted as a useful concept to get departments to break down internal barriers and cooperate fully, rather than try to duck responsibility for any shortcomings, and pass the buck whenever possible.

Teams cannot function without free and open communications between their members. Without communication there can be no team, only individuals, each doing their own thing. It is worth therefore considering for a moment what is needed to ensure good communications between team members. There are only two essentials –

- channels, or means of communicating, and
- motivation, or desire to communicate.

– and though one can compensate for the other to some extent, both must be adequate. If for instance you know from experience that a colleague is difficult to get hold of on the phone, but you have a strong desire to speak to him or her, you will persist. If however, the personal cost in terms of trying unsuccessfully to get through, becomes too high, you will probably give up, and the communication will fail. There will be longer term effects too: in future you may not even attempt to communicate because you expect it to be too much effort, and teamwork then becomes seriously weakened.

Now suppose the channels are adequate; you know that with portable phones, voice-mail and e-mail, one way or another you will get through. But let's suppose that in the past you have found communicating with your colleague to be unsatisfactory for one reason or another, then even though the channels are adequate, you probably won't communicate. You have to believe that your colleague will respect your views, value your comments and cooperate. If you know from experience that the most likely response will be stone-walling: 'We can't do anything about that,' – or buck passing: 'You'll have to speak to Fred,' – or just plain rejection: 'That's your problem, not ours,' – then are you going to bother communicating?

So the free flow of information within an organization doesn't just depend on the channels, the systems and the technology; it also depends on the culture, the willingness to work as a team, and the level of respect we hold for our colleagues.

Teamwork, you will remember from Chapter 1, is one of the cornerstones of TQM. Quality, as we have seen, is critically important to success, and yet some organizations still partly remove the responsibility for quality from those who produce the goods or services. They do this by setting up a quality control department which carries the can if a customer complains about quality. In fact, anyone who has any contact with the product or service can have an effect on quality. When different departments work to optimize their own separate objectives this can lead to a result which is far from satisfactory for the organization as a whole.

The Japanese avoid this pitfall. Their organizations seem to work well as teams, using quality circles (quality improvement teams) for instance to tap into the creativity and ingenuity of their workers. We will return to the subject of quality circles and their information needs in the next chapter when we examine kaizen tools, but for now let us observe that in the same way that a power shovel amplifies physical strength, so an information system to support teamwork should amplify the intellectual capacity of the team.

Software for group communications

The Lotus Development Corporation offers PC software designed to improve communications within groups, or teams of workers. They call it Lotus Notes. Here's what they say about it:

Innovative software for group communications that revolutionizes the way people work.

Lotus Notes is a first – software designed for the rapid development of work group applications within a networked environment. As networks connect PCs and workstations, Notes connects work groups. With Notes, people in work groups can share critical information – within a building, nationally, and internationally in different time-zones.

What's in it for you?

Lotus Notes is for people who need to share information, whether it be textual information, spreadsheets, graphics or images. Notes provides an environment where people can work together, no matter what physical barriers separate them. Through customized applications, Notes allows people to exchange information and ideas withou having to physically meet.

1 A Notes sales tracking application allows your sales team to stay active in the field, but still communicate and share vital up-to-date information with headquarters.
2 A Notes information newswire application keeps everyone informed of the latest business developments wherever they are in the world.
3 A Notes discussion database allows everyone to share information and exchange ideas without any physical meetings.

Notes adds value to an organization by harvesting the richest source of information it has – the knowledge of people within that organization. It increases the productivity of an organization because everyone is better informed and up-to-date with the latest developments.

Improved communications

Notes provides a single unifying platform that allows you seamlessly to join all of the basic types of business communication:

One to one	Electronic mail
One to many	Distribution lists, newsletters, reference libraries, newswires
Many to one	Executive information systems, tracking systems
Many to many	Discussion, group conferences

Lotus Notes software (see box) is designed for teamwork. It is not anywhere near as widely used as their spreadsheet product called 1-2-3. One reason is that Notes has not been around for as long as 1-2-3: it is a fairly new software product. Another reason may be more to do with organizational culture: western organizations tend to favour individualism, rather than cooperation and teamwork, and so products such as spreadsheets which are primarily designed for individuals to use are easier to sell than 'groupware'. This is likely to change, though, as old-style organizations re-shape or fade from the scene under pressure from newer, more flexible organizations.

Information for control

Teamwork and less centralized control may be desirable, but let us turn now to look at how many present-day organizations actually control their output.

Control system concepts

We need to define a few terms first. In control theory, we assume a 'system', which has a 'boundary'. 'Inputs' flow into a 'process' which changes them in some way and converts them into 'outputs' which flow out of the system (Figure 2.3).

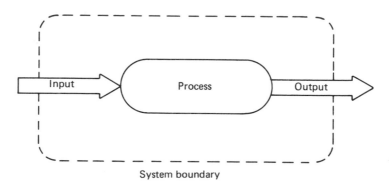

Figure 2.3   *Block diagram for a simple system*

A control system has another element, and that is something called 'feedback', where the output of the system is compared with some desired standard and if there is a difference, the input or the process is adjusted in some way to bring the output back into line (Figure 2.4).

We will touch upon systems again in Chapters 4 and 5; the concept of a system is important in this subject, so let's use a familiar example. Do you have a shower at home? If so, you may just have a hot and cold

Thin arrows show information flows

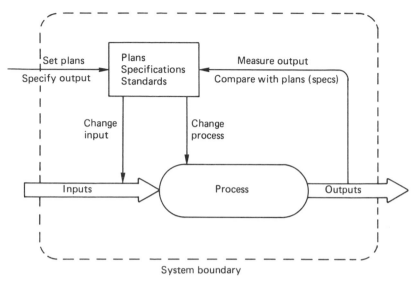

Figure 2.4 *Block diagram for a control system*

tap that you have to adjust to get the right temperature, or you may
have a thermostatically controlled unit.

A simple tap-controlled shower is a system for producing a mixture
of hot and cold water at the temperature you require, but it is not an
automatic control system. You have to do the controlling, so that when
someone turns on a tap somewhere else in the house, which affects the
balance of inputs to your system, you have to adjust the shower taps
to bring the temperature back within acceptable limits.

A thermostatically controlled shower is an automatic control system.
Before you step under the shower you provide an information input by
means of setting the control knob to the value, or standard required.
Then, the hot and cold supplies can vary, but providing they remain
within the design limits, the shower unit will automatically compensate for changes in the inputs, to provide a reasonably constant
output temperature. If the temperature of the hot water input falls, the
temperature of the output will begin to fall. But as soon as it does, the
unit detects that there is a difference between actual output and
planned output, increases the proportion of hot water in the input to
compensate, and brings the output back in line with the standard
(Figure 2.5).

To summarize, a simple control system has the following
elements:

- Input.
- A process for modifying the input in some way.
- Output.

Figure 2.5   *Control system for a shower*

- A standard to which the output should conform.
- Measurement of the output.
- Comparison of the output with the standard.
- Feedback.

Strictly speaking we should refer to this as negative feedback, because the adjustment to be made to the process or the inputs is always in the opposite direction to the error, and in proportion to the size of the error. For instance if the shower water is too hot, the input mixture is made cooler, and if it is very much too hot the input is made very much cooler.

Management control systems work in just the same way in principle. In production control for instance, if we have to produce 40,000 units in one month, and by the end of the first week we have produced 8,000, we know that we are 2,000 behind schedule because the plan requires 10,000 per week for four weeks. Negative feedback suggests that we should turn up the wick a bit – increase production because of the shortfall of actual production compared to the plan – by working overtime, or whatever means. Without early monitoring in this way, the error may get even worse and perhaps become irretrievable within the time remaining until the due date.

The routine collection of production information and comparing it against the plan is something to which computers are ideally suited, and was one of the first business applications of computers outside of the accounting and payroll functions, over twenty years ago.

Production control: materials requirement planning

Controlling the production of cars, or washing machines, or microwave ovens, involves more than just counting the number of finished items each week and then working some overtime if the number is less than planned. To put together a complex assembly of parts regularly and in large quantities involves detailed logistics to ensure the right quantities of components are available when required, and the right amounts of raw materials are available to make those components.

The software to handle these problems is called MRP software. It stands for materials requirement planning, and has three main inputs:

- the MPS or master production schedule.
- The BOM or bill of materials.
- The current inventory or level of stocks and their delivery lead-times, from the inventory file.

Remember, the purpose of MRP software is to achieve the master production schedule, but at the same time to control levels of raw materials and work-in-progress (WIP) so that stockouts do not occur.

The outputs consist of:

- Reports to production, telling what should be produced and when, and
- reports to purchasing, telling what to buy and when.

It works like this. The MPS (master production schedule) is determined by sales and marketing, partly from forecasted sales, and partly from orders received. It consists of a schedule of numbers of finished assemblies to be produced each week (Figure 2.6).

The BOM (bill of materials) for a product is a kind of structured parts list, in the form of a hierarchy, with the top level, level 0, being the finished assembly. The next level down, level 1, consists of the major sub-assemblies from which the final assembly is put together. Level 2 shows the parts from which the sub-assemblies are made, and

On-hand inventory at end of August = 100

Month	September				October				Nov	
Week No.	37	38	39	40	41	42	43	44	45	46
Forecast demand (gross requirements)	150	150	160	160	150	140	140	140	120	
Projected on-hand inventory (gross availability)	200	50	140	230	80	190	50	160	40	
Production planned (receipts) MPS	250		250	250		250		250		

To find projected on-hand inventory, add on-hand inventory for the preceding week to production planned for the current week. Then subtract forecast demand

Figure 2.6 *Master production schedule (MPS) for a table lamp*

Product structure diagram

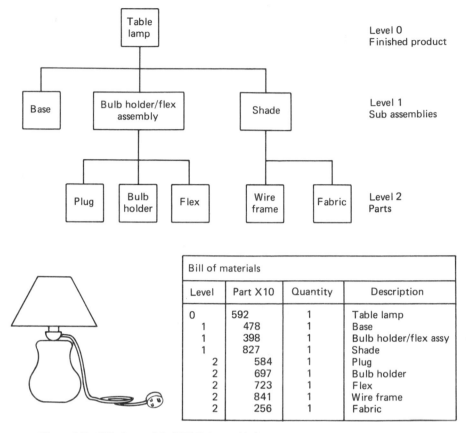

Figure 2.7 *Bill of materials (BOM) for a table lamp*

level 3 may be materials from which the parts are made. For instance a table lamp might have a BOM as in Figure 2.7.

You will probably realize that the BOM contains information on how the product is actually made. There are sometimes choices as to how the product is assembled and this will affect the BOM. For instance, should the plug be put on the flex before the flex is put on the lamp, or afterwards? Also, the greater the complexity of the final assembly, and the more operations there are to be performed, the greater the number of levels in the BOM. For instance if our table lamp manufacturer just puts together parts and sub-assemblies made by outside contractors, the BOM may only have three or four levels. If however, the company makes the parts in several stages from raw materials, builds them into sub-sub-assemblies, then sub-assemblies and final assemblies – then the BOM may have twice as many levels.

The third input to the MRP system is the inventory file, which keeps a tally of raw materials and work-in-progress, together with the lead-times for replenishment, either by making or buying from outside. The lead-times for manufacturing are of course influenced by the size of batch ordered. The software assumes a batch size which strikes a balance between the costs of holding large batches in stock, and the high costs of changing over the machines and losing productive capacity when many different small batches are planned.

When the MRP system is run, it produces from the master production schedule, a time-phased assembly schedule, by working backwards from the amounts required each week in the MPS. It takes into account the lead-times to find out when the sub-assemblies must be started if they are to be ready for final assembly. Then working backwards in time again, the software computes when the parts must be started if they are to be ready for making into sub-assemblies. And of course the materials must be ordered soon enough for them to arrive in time to be made into parts.

By chaining back like this, the software works out when to release purchase orders to suppliers, and works orders to the shop floor for manufacture.

In fact with just a simple product like a table lamp, a production assistant could probably keep tabs on the logistics. But in a manufacturing plant with a range of complex products, each with its own master production schedule, and some perhaps using the same sub-assemblies, the calculations rapidly become unmanageable without a computer.

Some disadvantages of MRP

MRP packages have been around for twenty years and more now. They were the only way we knew of handling the logistics of assembly for complex product ranges. However they require very heavy investment in hardware, software, maintenance and training. Typically it may take £500,000 to install, and take a year for an average size company to get up and running with MRP.

There are many different proprietary brands of MRP but most of them work in time units (called time buckets) of one week, and assume batch production. Taken together, these two factors mean that even though levels of inventory and work-in-progress are 'controlled', there must still be substantial amounts of WIP about for the system to function. So a company that installs MRP may be committing itself for the life of the system to working with substantial amounts of WIP. It may be possible to work with smaller rather than larger batch sizes, but even so this is not ideal at a time when firms are working towards systems of Just-in-time (JIT) production using batch sizes of one unit.

Working with a high level of WIP has several serious disadvantages:

- It ties up capital.
- It makes design changes difficult.

- It makes it difficult to adjust the throughput rate to match sudden changes in demand.
- It allows poor quality manufacture, whereas JIT will not. With JIT, the whole factory stops when a faulty part is produced – a strong incentive to produce zero defects.

Project control: critical path method

In manufacturing, controlling the flow of products is all-important. In the service sector it is teams and activities that must be coordinated and controlled. In both however, there are due-dates to be met, and just as in manufacturing, MRP is used to work back from the due-date to find out when to start work on products, so in the service sector a similar technique can be used to determine when activities should be scheduled to start and finish. The group of techniques are called network analysis or critical path analysis. If you work in the service sector, I hope you will not be too dismayed to learn that this technique also originated in the manufacturing sector, but it has been found to be just as useful in the service sector.

The story starts back in the 1950s when after the Second World War several very large projects were being started, mainly in the States, and these were presenting new problems of coordination and planning. It is in the nature of projects that they last only for a period of time, during which many different teams and types of activity have to be coordinated and brought to a successful conclusion by the due-date. Separate groups of researchers were addressing these problems and they came up with several variants of essentially the same technique, the best known of which is PERT. PERT was used to control the US Navy's Polaris Missile development programme and was credited with bringing forward the completion date by two whole years.

Few managers get involved with projects as big as Polaris, but PERT can be just as effective in controlling smaller projects such as launching a new service or product, installing a computer system and training staff to use it, or launching a sales training programme.

Here's a simple example to illustrate how it works. Suppose you are in charge of a team responsible for arranging a management training programme for your organization, to start soon. You have listed all the component activities, and their durations in days:

List locations	2
Select locations	4
Plan topics	3
Get speakers	7
Arrange speaker travel plans	5
Design and print brochure	14
Final check on travel plans	8
Take reservations	6
Run training programme	10

The technique has three phases:

- The planning phase when it is decided what activities will make up the project, and the order in which they must be completed.
- The analysis phase when the activities are laid out in their logical order in the form of a network of arrows, each with its own duration, so that each can be scheduled to start and finish at the appropriate time.
- The control phase when the project is running, and must be held to plan.

Planning

In our example, the planning phase is complete, and the results are shown in the table above.

Analysis

In the analysis phase, these activities must be shown as a network. Each activity is represented by an arrow, and initially, the durations are ignored. The arrows are laid out in the form of a network because some activities are dependent on earlier preceding activities, whereas other activities are independent and can be done in parallel (Figure 2.8).

In our example for instance, speaker travel plans cannot be arranged until the locations have been finalized. This is a dependent relationship. It is OK though for the speaker travel plans to be arranged at the same time as the brochure is being prepared, because these activities are independent. When the network has been drawn the durations can be put on, and the overall project duration calculated. It is determined by the longest chain of activities through the network which of course is called the critical path.

Control

If a critical activity is delayed by so much as a day, the whole project will be delayed by the same amount, whereas non-critical activities lying on shorter chains through the network will have more time available for their completion than is strictly necessary. Typically perhaps only a quarter of all the activities in a project may turn out to be critical, and that is what makes this technique so popular with managers. It allows you to focus your limited time and attention on those activities where it will be most effective.

During this control phase it is important to make sure everyone knows when they are working on critical activities, and the importance of sticking to schedule. Networks however are not very useful for communicating information, and so scheduling information is usually

Figure 2.8 *Network of activities for organizing a management training programme*

extracted from the network and shown on a Gantt chart – a horizontal bar chart – which everyone understands (Figure 2.9).

However, the network forms the basis for planning and re-planning as the inevitable contingencies arise during the life of the project.

Needless to say, computers are now making the whole process much easier. Several quite powerful packages for the serious user are available from about £500. After keying in the activity data, the computer performs the analysis and presents the control information in whatever form you require – as a network, a bar chart or as tables of figures.

Some names of commonly used software are: Plantrac II from Computerline Ltd, SuperProject Expert from Computer Associates, Project Manager Workbench from Hoskyns and Artemis from Metier. There are many other excellent packages around, too numerous to mention them all.

Figure 2.9 *Gantt chart of activities for organizing a management training programme*

Competence self-assessment

Here are some questions to help you consolidate what you have learned from this chapter, and relate it to your own experience at work.

1

Under the headings of 'Regular' and 'Occasional', list the channels and types of communication you receive while doing your job. For instance, a regular channel through which you will probably receive information is the phone, and possibly the type of information might be sales enquiries.

2

List the main activities that occupied you at work last week, or during a typical week. Estimate the percentages of your time during that week which you spent on each of the following activities: strategic planning, management control, and operational control. From this analysis, would R. N. Anthony classify you as a junior, a middle or a senior manager?

3

Give an example of a decision you often have to make at work with inadequate information. What extra information would make the decision easier or safer? What can you do to arrange for more information to be available next time?

4

Who inside your organization receives work that you do? Do you regard them as your customers? If you were to ask them how you could improve the quality of service or product that you deliver to them, how would they answer?

5

Are you required to operate to an annual budget? Do you have regular monthly or quarterly budget reviews? If so, use systems terminology to describe these features as parts of a financial control system.

6

Table 2.1 lists in the first column the seven activities making up a complete project. In the second column are the activities that immediately precede each activity, and in the third column are the durations of each activity in weeks.

(a) Draw the network for these activities. (You don't need the durations for this.) Also, remember that the activity letters should be put on the activity arrows, not the event circles. Make sure all the arrows point forwards to the right.

(b) Divide each event circle with a vertical line. Now do a forward pass through the network, starting at the first event on the left and working to the right. Put in the earliest time each event can occur on the left half of each event circle. Remember that an event cannot

Table 2.1

Activity reference	Depends on	Duration
A	–	2
B	–	5
C	–	1
D	B	10
E	A, D	3
F	C	6
G	E, F	8

occur until all routes through to that event have been completed. Thus the earliest event time for each event is equal to the length of the longest route through to that event.

(c) What is the shortest time that the project can be completed in? It is the same as the earliest event time for the last event on the right.

(d) Now fill in the latest event times by doing a backward pass, starting at the last event on the right and working back towards the left. Put the latest event times in the right half of each event circle. The final event on the right will have a latest event time equal to its earliest event time if the project is to be completed in the shortest possible period. The penultimate event(s) will have a latest event time equal to the latest event time of the final event less the duration of the activity in between. If there is more than one path leading back to an earlier event, it is the longest path that should be used to find its latest event time.

(f) Mark up the critical path. It is easily recognized as the sequence of activities linking all the events which have their earliest event time equal to their latest event time.

7

A promoter wishes to present a summer concert in the gardens of a mansion near Oxford. She decides to use PERT to help manage the project, and the time estimates for the activities are as shown in Table 2.2.

Table 2.2

Activity reference	Description	Immediate predecessor	Time estimate (days)
A	Select musicians	–	5
B	Contracts with agents	A	10
C	Arrange travel and accommodation	B	14
D	Radio, adverts, promotion	B	7
E	Print tickets, programmes	B	6
F	Sell tickets	D, E	21
G	Confirm travel and accommodation	C	11
H	Hire ticket sellers	C	16
J	Rehearsals	H	2
K	Present concert	G, F, J	3

(a) Draw the network for the project and indicate which activities lie on the critical path.
(b) What is the shortest time that the project can be completed in? How might knowing this be useful to the organizer?
(c) If the project is delayed, it may be necessary to reduce the project duration by shortening an activity. One such proposal is to contract out the ticket selling so that activity H takes only 1 day. What effect would this have on the expected project duration?

8

Prepare a critical path network for the following activities involved in the preparation of a ham sandwich. Assume you have as many helpers as necessary. Determine the critical path, and calculate what the shortest

Table 2.3

Activity	Duration (seconds)
Get bread from bin	60
Unwrap and cut two slices of bread	50
Get ham from refrigerator	40
Cut one slice of ham	50
Get mustard from cupboard and prepare	240
Put mustard in assembled sandwich	40
Get butter from refrigerator	80
Put butter on two slices of bread	70
Assemble two buttered slices and ham	40
Cut sandwich in two and serve	40

'project' time will be. Of all the activities originating from the first event in the network, which one could have the latest starting time? How late could it start? (See Table 2.3.)

9

A manufacturer of consumer electronics, in conjuction with an advertising agency, is planning an advertising project to launch a new personal computer. The project will involve newspaper and television advertising and will conclude with a press conference. The project activities are shown in Table 2.4.

Draw a network for the advertising project. Show which activities are critical. What is the total project duration?

The agency wishes to shorten the overall project time, and is considering the following ideas:
(a) The photographs for the newspaper advertisements can be taken while the accompanying text is being written.
(b) By allocating extra resources, the duration for agreeing the film contract can be shortened.

Table 2.4

Activity	Description	Time (weeks)	Depends on
A	Plan campaign	2	–
B	Contracts with newspapers	3	A
C	Write text	3	A
D	Take photographs	4	C
E	Prepare artwork	2	D
F	Artwork to newspapers	1	B, E
G	Contract with film maker	3	A
H	Contracts with TV companies	3	A
J	Write film script	4	A
K	Make film	6	J, G
L	Film to TV company	1	H, K
M	Arrange press conference	2	F, L

(c) By allocating extra resources, the duration for making the film can be shortened. Which one of these should the agency choose in order to shorten the project? How many weeks can be saved?

References and further reading

Anthony, R. N., Dearden J. and Bedford, N. M. (1990). *Management Control Systems* (5th edn). Richard D. Irwin Inc.

Lucey, T. *Management Information Systems* (6th edn). D.P Publications.

Belasco, J. A. (1990). *Teaching the Elephant to Dance. Empowering change in your organization.* Hutchinson Business Books.

Schonberger, Knod (1991). *Operations Management. Improving customer service* (4th edn). Irwin.

Project Management Today. Monthly magazine published by Larchdrift Projects Ltd.

3 Information and personal effectiveness

Why is this chapter relevant?

Do you want to be a better manager? There are some simple techniques described here which can help you use information to make better decisions, and communicate better with your colleagues. Decision-making and communication are functions that lie at the very heart of management. By learning these techniques, your competence as a manager will immediately benefit.

How to analyse and present information effectively

You, as a manager must achieve results through people. The only way you can do this is by communicating with them, that is, giving them information. If you favour – and can get away with – an autocratic management style, the information you give may be in the form of instructions. Nowadays however, it is much more likely that you will have to persuade your staff to work the way you want by selling them ideas, rather than telling them what to do, but this need not be difficult. Very often, by presenting the facts in an obvious format, the ideas will sell themselves. Then, appropriate action is easy to see and nobody needs telling what to do. Most people will obey what Mary Parker Follet called 'the law of the situation' and just get on and do it.

Most of the techniques that will be described are very simple: anyone can understand and use them. They consist of little more than structured ways of displaying information. You can use them, and you should encourage your staff to use them. When the Japanese have demonstrated how effective they can be, it is a mystery to me why more western organizations do not make greater use of them. Have we more of our fair share of flat-earthers, or do we just have inadequate levels of management training?

This article first appeared in 'Management News', the newspaper of Oxford Polytechnic School of Business, in Spring 1992.

Kaizen Tools

Know what these are? If you work for Nissan in Sunderland you would do because all employees – not just managers – are given their own Kaizen Manual explaining what they are and how to use them. The word kaizen is Japanese but the tools themselves with one exception were all invented in the west, and they are essential to the process of improvement. Indeed without their widespread use it would have been impossible for Japan to rise phoenix-like from the nuclear ashes of World War 2 to her present dominant position in many world markets. The tools include:

- Pie, bar and scatter diagrams.
- Pareto diagrams.
- Ishikawa diagrams.
- The normal curve, and standard deviation $\bar{X}$ and R charts.

Japanese employees at all levels organized in small groups called quality circles use these tools routinely to analyse and improve their work. The many small improvements being initiated everywhere result in a never-ending, relentless advance. That is what the word kaizen means – a constant gradual universal process of improvement. It is like a religion: a shared commitment to find a better future.

Of course kaizen tools on their own won't guarantee a one-way ticket to success in world markets, but they are essential for a proper scientific, analytical approach which along with teamwork and an obsession with quality, form the basis of total quality management, the western equivalent of kaizen. TQM consultants Joiner Associates of Wisconsin USA promote the idea by means of the Joiner triangle shown in Figure 3.1.

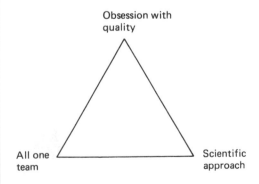

Figure 3.1 *The Joiner triangle*

Teamwork and an obessesion with quality in an organization require major cultural changes which can only be started by the chief executive, but anyone can use a scientific approach to make changes based on sound evidence. And that's where the kaizen tools come in: they're reliable methods for analysing evidence.

So is this scientific management all over again – F. W. Taylor's discredited ideas of seventy years ago?' It is true that Elton Mayo's famous experiments at the Hawthorne Works of Western Electric, Illinois, showed that treating humans like machines just doesn't work, but some of Taylor's approach did survive in Work Study and Ergonomics. The scientific method is OK; it is the way we apply it that we sometimes get wrong. After all, scientists of every discipline used it very effectively for 300 years before Taylor came along.

The scientific method was first proposed by philosopher and former Lord Chancellor Francis Bacon during the reign of King James Ist. He argued that you can't deduce everything about the universe just from logic without experimenting. Later, others including Isaac Newton refined the method which basically has four steps:

1 Observe an effect,
2 guess its cause,
3 test your theory by experimenting, and thus
4 prove a relationship between cause and effect.

However there are critics who say that even science doesn't operate strictly according to this method and besides, for busy managers it all sounds a bit too academic. That's why ninety-one year-old quality guru Dr Deming proposed the PDCA or Plan-Do-Check-Amend cycle which the Japanese have taken to heart and used to such effect, and why IBM uses a similar 4-step cycle: Analyse-Solve-Implement-Maintain, as part of their Market Driven Quality programme. These cycles and the one used by 'learning organizations', Question-Theory-Test-Reflection, are all loosely based on Bacon's original supposition, and they all require evidence to be analysed and small experiments or tests to be carried out, to discover how to improve. This is what the kaizen tools are for.

Pie, bar and scatter diagrams

In the UK we use these for reports and presentations. But in TQM organizations, quality circles use them to analyse evidence and gain insight into problems. See Figure 3.2.

Pareto diagrams

Vilfredo Pareto, the Italian economist, showed that it was common for about 20 per cent of nationals to own about 80 per cent of the wealth of a nation. These proportions crop up in many other circumstances too. Quality circles use the diagrams for 80/20

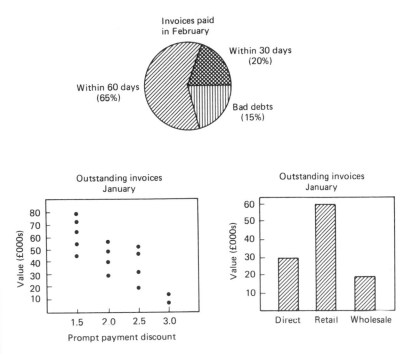

Figure 3.2 *Pie, scatter and bar diagrams*

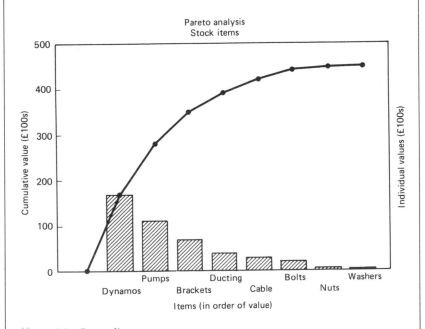

Figure 3.3 *Pareto diagram*

analysis to rank items and separate the vital few items from amongst the many other items which are also important, but less so. It is a simple but powerful technique for focusing your attention where it can be most effective. See Figure 3.3.

Ishikawa diagrams

The Japanese professor Kaouru Ishikawa invented these which are also known as cause-effect diagrams, or fishbone diagrams as shown in Figure 3.4. They help quality circles to develop a comprehensive view of factors which might influence a problem.

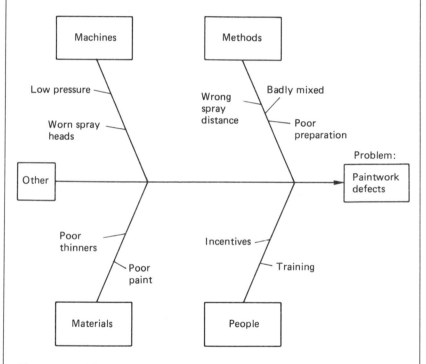

Figure 3.4 *Ishikawa diagram*

Normal curve and standard deviation

These are fundamental to the study of variation. If you are serious about improving quality, you have no option but to get familiar with the Normal curve and its standard deviation. Why? Because top quality is impossible with high variation and to reduce variation is the same as to improve quality. High variation means low predictability. If a product or service varies each time you supply it, your customers can't know what to expect, and quality assurance is all about meeting and exceeding your customers' expectations. For instance in a supermarket, shopping can take just twenty minutes – or as much as an hour if long queues form. This is high variation and low predictability, which most customers will seek to avoid. Some will shop elsewhere to avoid the risk of an hour-long ordeal, even when shopping takes longer on average. (See Figure 3.5.)

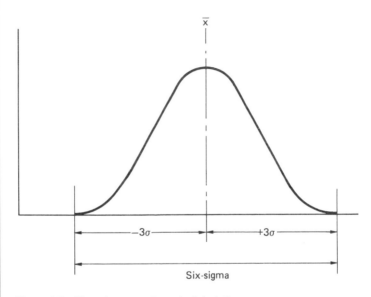

Figure 3.5 *Normal curve and standard deviation*

Variation can be of two types: that due to a single, special, assignable cause, and that due to many common, unassignable causes which usually cancel out but occasionally stack up one way or the other. Unfortunately in practice it is difficult to tell the two apart, and if you treat a chance stacking up of common causes believing it to be a special cause – or vice versa – you will actually increase the amount of variation and make the situation worse! For example suppose you are in a rifle target shooting competition and you want to maximize your score with five shots. If you were to fire all five shots without adjusting the sights you wouldn't expect all the shots to go through the same hole in the target; there will be some natural variation due to common causes, and the shots will form a group of five holes – not too far apart, one hopes. Now suppose you start the competition knowing that your sights are reasonably well but perhaps not perfectly adjusted, and the first shot falls a little to the left of the bullseye.

You could adjust the sights to compensate before firing the next shot, and continue like that each time compensating for the error of the previous shot. Or, you could fire all five shots without adjusting the sights, and in fact this will result in a tighter grouping and a higher score.

Treating common cause variation as if it were a special cause is what Dr Deming refers to as tampering with the process. In business a manager who makes an immediate adjustment to procedures because a single customer has complained, is tampering. The knee-jerk reaction of the macho manager usually does more harm than good in the long run. Many UK managers don't understand these statistical concepts: all Nissan employees are encouraged to learn about them.

X-bar and R charts

These can be used for monitoring our processes for supplying services and products. The average and range within samples of five are charted, making it possible to distinguish between common and special causes, and detect even slight changes in a process before it results in out-of-spec output. The charts are simple to use, but do require some statistical knowledge to set up. You may hear the term 'six-sigma' bandied about by employees from IBM, Motorola and other TQM companies. What they are referring to is the range of common cause variation which is controlled by using $\bar{X}$ and R charts, as shown in Figure 3.6.

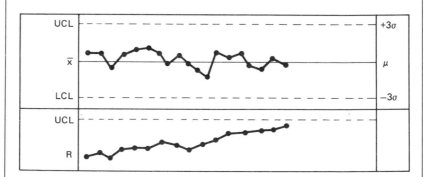

Figure 3.6   *X-bar and R-charts*

These then are some of the kaizen tools needed to support the myriad of small experiments which should be going on at all levels everywhere in your organization if it is to keep up with rising customer expectations.

Survival is not a foregone conclusion, as some big world airlines are discovering during this recession. But British Airways who were in deep trouble in 1981, losing £200 per minute through that year, became profitable in 1984 following the decision of chief executive Sir Colin Marshall to introduce TQM, and as the world's favourite airline, it is still profitable even in the current difficult conditions.

Sir Colin encourages everyone to make small experiments, recognizing that many of these will fail, but will always add to knowledge. The organizational culture must support experimentation: people must be prepared to take small risks and not be afraid of the errors that come with trial and error. That is why Sir Colin's slogan is 'Practise walking on water on shallow ponds.'

Communicating information

A technical model of communication is often portrayed as in Figure 3.7. This simple model has three stages:

- A sender prepares and transmits . . .
- a message via some medium to . . .
- a receiver who receives and understands the message, thus completing the communication process.

Or does it?

A managerial model of communication should have a fourth stage: action. The essence of management is getting results through people. It is not enough therefore, if the receivers of your message just receive and understand it. They must behave differently in some desired way from how they would otherwise have behaved. That is the ultimate test of effectiveness.

So how can you improve your chances of securing action? Well, you must design your message to achieve two things when it is received:

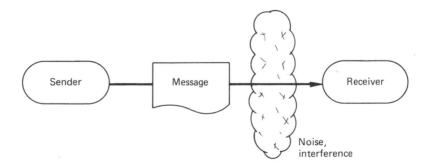

Figure 3.7 *A model of the communication process*

● It must be understood, so keep your message simple, uncluttered, and free from ambiguities or uncertainties.
● It must be interesting and relevant to your readers.

Authors on the subject generally agree that effective communication is very difficult to achieve. When figures are a significant part of the message, it adds an extra difficulty, so don't be discouraged if you find it hard.

Whenever you communicate, you are selling – you want your audience to take some kind of action in the same way as the sales person wants the prospect to reach for his or her chequebook. Organizations function more effectively when managers view other managers in their organization as internal customers for their services. If you want to be a better manager, learn to be a better 'ideas salesperson'.

Using the kaizen tools

Like any skill, practice makes perfect, and doing something for the first time is always the most difficult. Remember when you first learned to ride a bike? But now you know you can go back and ride one anytime, even if you haven't been near a bike for years.

When you learned how to ride, you watched someone else do it first, then had a go yourself. So in that tradition, here are some examples of how to use the kaizen tools, with lots of help and detailed guidance each step of the way. In the self-assessment section at the end of this chapter you will find exercises with less help, for you to test your understanding.

You can follow through the examples here and copy them yourself first if you wish, or if you prefer, just read through and then try the exercises. You can do them manually or by computer. The computer instructions are fairly general as the specific keystrokes necessary for achieving various effects will vary according to the particular spreadsheet available to you. Where it is necessary to give specific examples I have assumed that an up-to-date version of Lotus 1-2-3 is available.

If you are unfamiliar with PCs and spreadsheets, do the exercises manually and read Chapter 4 first, before trying to follow the computer instructions in this chapter.

How to draw a pie chart

This is ideal for breaking down a grand total and showing the proportions of its components. For instance:

● Total sales, made up from northern, Midlands, southern, and export divisions.

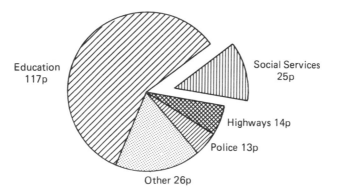

Spending £1.95 a day for each adult

Figure 3.8   *The pie chart*

- Total council spending, on education, social services, highways etc.
- Total costs, on labour, materials, transport, overheads etc.

You should try to restrict yourself to four or five slices at most, or the chart will become cluttered with detail and lose impact. (See Figure 3.8.) The detail is better presented as a table later on for those who are interested.

By computer

The easiest way is to use a PC with spreadsheet software. With Lotus 1-2-3 for instance, all you need do is list on the spreadsheet grid the component names and their values in two adjacent columns. Then tell the computer how you want the information displayed: choose the graph option, and select 'pie' as the type. Then set the names as the X-range and the values as the A-range. That's all there is to it; you can now view the pie chart on screen to check it looks OK, and then print it.

If you wish, you can add some embellishments: a two-line title, and choose different cross-hatching, or colours for the slices. You can even pull out slightly one or more slices of the pie, or even make slices disappear.

You will need to learn the specific keyboard presses to invoke these commands, but that is not difficult, and like riding a bicycle, once learned, you tend not to forget it.

Manually

To prepare a pie chart manually though is awkward because you need some drawing instruments which may not be to hand. The minimum you need are a pencil, a ruler, a pair of compasses, and a protractor. (You may have to raid your daughter's or son's pencil case for the protractor!) A calculator would be useful too. The steps are as follows:

1 Draw a circle
2 Calculate the angle for the first slice. To do this you calculate the proportion of the total that the first component represents, and work out this proportion of 360 degrees. For instance, suppose you have the following figures:

Fixed costs	250
Variable costs	270
Overheads	230
Total	750

The whole pie represents the 750, and each slice must be sized in proportion. The first slice is the fixed costs of 250. These are one-third of the total 750, and so you need to draw a slice which is one-third of the whole pie circle – in other words, one-third of 360 degrees, which is 120 degrees.
3 Now draw the slice for these fixed costs, by first drawing a radius from the centre of the circle to the right until it touches the outside of the circle. Now use your protractor to measure 120 degrees round the circle from this radius and draw a second radius. Label this slice 'fixed costs'. See Figure 3.9.
4 Next calculate the size of the second slice, as follows:

$$(270/750) \times 360 = 129.6$$

The second slice should be 129.6 degrees, but 130 degrees is perfectly close enough. Again, measure 130 degrees round the pie from your

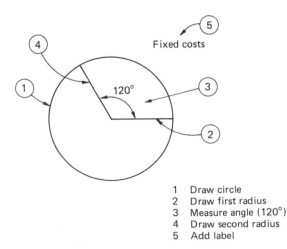

1   Draw circle
2   Draw first radius
3   Measure angle (120°)
4   Draw second radius
5   Add label

Figure 3.9   *Drawing a pie charge, stage 1*

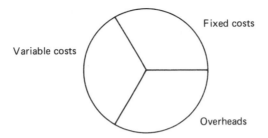

Figure 3.10   *Drawing a pie charge, stage 2*

second radius and draw in the third radius. Label this slice 'variable costs', and the remainder of the pie 'overheads' (Figure 3.10).

And that's it; the pie chart is finished. You can jazz it up a bit to make it more visually interesting by adding a title and colouring it in if you wish, but don't make it too complicated. The essence of good commmunication is to keep things simple (Figure 3.11).

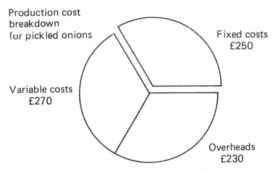

Figure 3.11   *Drawing a pie charge, stage 3*

How to draw a bar chart

Let's use the same figures we used for the pie chart.

By computer

Once again, with a PC this is a breeze, especially if you have already done the pie chart exercise, because you will already have set the parameters. All you need do is change the graph type from 'Pie' to 'Bar' – and that's it, your bar chart is done, ready for viewing on screen or printing.

Manually

Manually too, the bar chart is easier to do than the pie chart. You need a vertical scale up to a nice round figure larger than the largest component. 300 is suitable for our example. Then, just draw vertical bars at the appropriate height against the scale. (See Figure 3.12.)

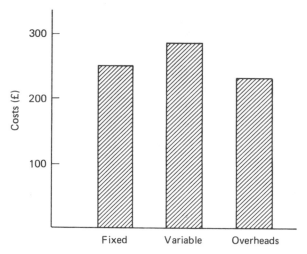

Figure 3.12 *Drawing a bar chart*

How to draw a scatter diagram

This type of chart is useful for investigating whether, or showing that there is a relationship between two different measurements. For instance you may wish to investigate whether monthly sales tend to increase when you increase your monthly spend on advertising. You should expect some kind of positive relationship. (Positive means when one increases, the other does too. Negative means one decreases as the other increases.) However, the relationship may not necessarily be perfectly clear, as other factors can influence sales as well as advertising. Bad weather can have a negative effect and so can your competitors' spending on advertising, whereas a fall in interest rates may have a positive effect. These other external influences – uncontrolled variables – tend to obscure the effect of your advertising and sometimes it is only by charting sales against advertising that we can demonstrate a positive relationship.

When preparing a scatter diagram you should always put the controlled variable – advertising in this case – along the bottom, or x-axis. The dependent variable, sales, will then rise or fall against the vertical y-axis.

By computer

With your PC and spreadsheet software you should now have some idea of how to get started. The steps are:

1 Prepare the month date (just for reference), advertising spend, and sales as three adjacent columns on your spreadsheet.

2 Now set the range of values in the advertising spend column as the x-range. These values will then appear along the bottom of the chart, and we would expect the monthly sales to go up as we move along the bottom axis from the lower values on the left to the higher ones on the right.
3 Now set the range of values in the monthly sales column as the y-range. Lotus actually allows you to have up to six different y-ranges all on the same graph, referred to as the A, B, C, D, E and F ranges. Choose the A-range for monthly sales.
4 Set the graph type to XY and use 'Options' to turn off the lines which by default the computer will use to connect up the points. You just want a symbol to appear at each point – and there you have it. The scatter graph is done, and if there is a positive relationship, the scatter of points should reveal an obvious trend upwards and to the right, with higher values of sales being associated with higher values of advertising, as shown in Figure 3.13.

Figure 3.13 *Drawing a scatter diagram*

Manually

Manually the procedure is much the same, except you have to use pencil and ruler to produce the axes, and chart the points on the graph by hand. There is nothing very difficult about this; it is just a bit time consuming, and the quality of the results depends on your skill and patience. Remember it doesn't matter in what order you plot the points so long as you don't forget any of them. All you are trying to show is that higher values of sales are associated with higher values of advertising, month by month, whenever they occur.

How to draw a Pareto diagram

This is a really simple technique which allows you to focus in on the few critical factors amongst the many other important ones. There are basically three simple steps:

● Rank items in order of value.
● Work out their proportions of the total, (just as you did for the pie chart).
● Plot a running total.

– and if that is too difficult you can even get away with just ranking the items in order of value and plotting them as a bar chart.

Once again, the PC and spreadsheet make the task easy, at least to produce a passable likeness to a Pareto diagram. But first, the background: let's see where the technique came from.

Vilfredo Pareto was an Italian economist who in 1896 attempted to show that income is not randomly distributed in any society, but that the bulk of all income is concentrated in the hands of a fairly small proportion of receivers.

When he plotted the percentage of income against the percentage of the population receiving the income, he came up with a curve of characteristic shape which, as is the case with the Normal Distribution curve, has since been found to crop up in a variety of different situations. The curve is shown in Figure 3.14 and is variously known as a Pareto curve, a Lorenz curve, 80/20 analysis, and ABC analysis.

The object of the analysis is to isolate the 'vital few' from the 'less important many'. In the field of stock control for instance, most

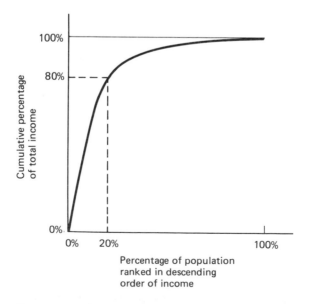

Figure 3.14 *The Pareto curve*

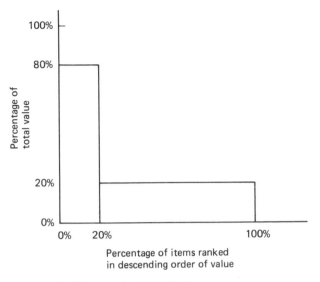

Figure 3.15 *Pareto analysis simplified*

factories place a large number of small orders and a small number of large orders. A simplified picture is shown in Figure 3.15, where 80 per cent of the money spent goes on only 20 per cent of the orders placed, the rest of the orders accounting for only 20 per cent of the expenditure. It is easy to overlook this fact, and there is a natural tendency to spend almost as much administrative effort on small purchase orders as on large ones. Adopting one standard form and procedure for every purchase amounts to administrative overkill on cheap items, while falling short on the largest non-repeating orders.

Pareto analysis can be used in any situation where you want to focus in on the few key factors of a particular problem, from amongst the many other rather less important factors. Here are some situations where Pareto may be useful:

- Cost analysis – to pick out the highest cost items, or operations, or processes, or elements.
- Time analysis – to pick out the few most time consuming operations, or processes.
- Scrap or wastage analysis – to pick out the main causes for high scrap rates.
- Breakdown analysis – to discover the main causes for machine breakdowns.
- Quality failures – to analyse these and find where or how most of them occur.

Manually

Here is an example to see how you would do it manually. Suppose you wish to analyse the causes of downtime on a production line. We know the minutes lost due to each of the various causes. They are shown in Figure 3.16. The procedure is as follows:

1 List the causes in order of importance, starting with the cause of most lost time, in a table with column 1 containing the causes and column 2 showing the minutes lost.
2 In column 3, list the running total of minutes lost. The last value in this column will be the total downtime.
3 In column 4, take each running total in column 3 and express it as a percentage of the total downtime (Figure 3.17).
4 Now chart the running total of percentages against the reasons listed along the bottom axis ranked in order of largest first (Figure 3.18).
5 By looking at the curve, you can now split it into two sections: the first 20 per cent of reasons (about three, Electrical, Mechanical and Parts in this case) account for nearly 80 per cent of the total minutes lost and the remaining 80 per cent of reasons together only total about 20 per cent of the total. If you wish, you can split the range into three sections, A, B and C. The A reasons are the most

Reasons for down time	Minutes lost
Tool breakages	1
Repairs	10
Operator absent	2
Low air pressure	3
Fire alarm	6
Mechanical faults	34
Electrical faults	82
Interlock open	1
Parts shortages	18
Accidents	4

Figure 3.16 *Pareto example: causes of down-time and time lost*

Cause	Minutes lost	Running total	Cum. % of total
Electrical faults	82	82	51
Mechanical faults	34	116	72
Parts shortages	18	134	83
Repairs	10	144	89
Fire alarm	6	150	93
Accidents	4	154	96
Low air pressure	3	157	97
Operator absent	2	159	98
Tool breakages	1	160	99
Interlock open	1	161	100

Total minutes lost 161

Figure 3.17 *Pareto example: arranging the values*

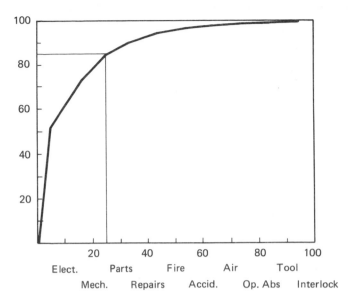

Figure 3.18   *Pareto example: drawing the curve*

important, lying on the steep part of the curve, and the C reasons the least important, on the flat part at the top. The B reasons as you might expect are the ones in the transitional range in between.

We now know that electrical faults are the main cause of lost time, even though it may turn out that they don't occur very often. If this is the case, by preventing just one or two electrical faults we can make a big reduction in downtime.

By computer

Using the PC and Lotus, it is not possible to produce a histogram – that is, a bar chart with the bars next to each other and touching, with no space between. But if you are prepared to overlook the spaces between the bars, you can produce your Pareto analysis as follows:

1 List your items by name in the first column of your spreadsheet.
2 Put the values against each name in the second column.
3 Rank the items in order of descending value – in other words, largest first, then next largest and so on. Your PC will do this for you in a flash: just use the /Data Sort command. Press the Help key (usually the <F1> key) for a more detailed explanation.
4 We now want to produce the running totals, so in the first row of the third column, repeat the value in the same row of column 2. Then in the next row of the third column, i.e. in cell C3, write a little formula

to add the next value in column 2 to the first value in column 3. In our example using Lotus, it should be +C2+B3. This will then automatically bring the running total into cell C3. Then using just a few keystrokes, you can copy this formula into all the remaining cells in column 3 and the running total values will appear instantly.

5 Now in column 4 we need to display the proportions of the total that each of the values in column 3 represent. With Lotus that's easy. The total at the foot of column 3 is 161 minutes, so we just take each value and divide it by 161 and multiply by 100 to show it as a percentage. In practice, you should put in cell D2 the following formula: +C2/161*100. Then just copy this formula into the rest of the column. The proportions – percentages actually – appear instantly.

6 The final step is to display the information graphically. Select the /Graph command and set the items in column 1 as the x-range, along the x-axis. Then you should set the range for the the running total of proportions in column D. Set this as the A-range and select to display it as a line graph. In fact you have to over-ride the default settings to get it to display as a Pareto curve. Do this by manually setting the lower and upper values of the A-range to 0 and 100. Also you have to introduce a row of zeros across the top of columns A to D, making sure they are included in the X- and B-ranges, so that the curve starts off at the origin of the graph.

7 You can also display the values in the B column in the form of a bar chart. They will appear ranked, largest at the left, declining progressively to smallest on the right. Again using the /Graph command, set the values in the B column as the B-range and select to display it as a bar chart against the same X-range as before. With later versions of Lotus you can get both displays to appear together. You can even have two different y-scales – values up the left side, and percentages up the right, or vice versa. You cannot make it look quite right though; it is one of the shortcomings of Lotus that you cannot produce true histograms. You have to put up with the spaces between the bars.

How to draw an Ishikawa diagram

Here's another simple technique with a fancy name. In fact it is so simple you might question whether it can really be of any value. In the West we tend to undervalue simple ideas. This is certainly true of some academics who secretly feel a need to set themselves apart from lesser mortals; an idea is not worth their attention if it is easy to teach and understand. Simple but powerful ideas can sometimes be excluded from syllabuses on the grounds that they are not intellectually demanding enough. Anyway this one got through the net.

A problem-solving tool for use by groups

The Ishikawa diagram is named after its originator Dr Kaoru Ishikawa, a Japanese professor who, along with Deming and Juran was in at the beginning of Japan's quality revolution during the 1950s. He suggested that groups called quality circles should use this diagram, also called a fishbone or cause-effect diagram, for problem solving, and identifying cause and effect relationships.

The diagram is different from some of the other techniques because it is not much use in reports and the like, for communicating information. It is more of an informal tool to provide a focus for the group, in producing a comprehensive review of all possible causes of some observed effect. It is a useful tool for a group leader working on a markerboard to collect and categorize ideas.

Quality circles, or quality improvement groups as they are sometimes called, are of course concerned with the quality of product or

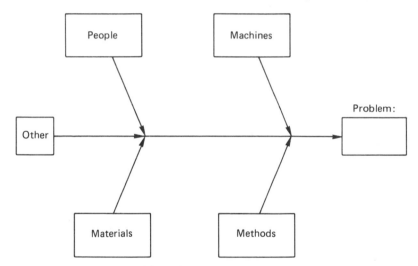

Figure 3.19   *Starting an Ishikawa diagram*

service. The four major categories that can have an impact on quality are humans (Men), Machines, Materials and Methods – known as the 4Ms – and these usually form four of the 'bones' along with a catch-all fifth bone labelled 'Other'. A generic structure for you as a group leader to use on your markerboard in analysing a quality problem should look like that in Figure 3.19. You then add little bones to these five main bones for subsidiary causes under each of the five categories.

Obviously a PC is no use for preparing Ishikawa diagrams, and it is difficult even to suggest a rigid procedure for using this informal tool. Another example might help, however, and so here is an Ishikawa diagram produced by a quality circle while they were discussing a problem of customers in a restaurant complaining that food was cold. (See Figure 3.20.)

Figure 3.20 *Using the Ishikawa diagram: reviewing causes of complaint*

The Ishikawa diagram can be used by any problem-solving group interested in determining causes and effects. It should not be reserved just for quality problems, and the main bones need not necessarily be just the 4Ms. It can be used as an informal, flexible tool wherever appropriate.

The normal curve and standard deviation

In contrast to the earlier techniques, to get the most from this subject you need to know some elementary statistics. We cannot go into that here so I shall restrain myself and just describe the main properties of the normal curve and the way it is used.

So what is this curve? It is a bell-shaped curve which crops up in all sorts of situations wherever variation occurs. It often arises when we plot a frequency histogram of a scatter of results about some central value, so let's take a look at histograms to start with.

Frequency histograms

6	10	9	13	11
12	8	8	1	9
7	3	12	10	9
15	7	10	9	8

A table of data like this makes my eyes glaze over – how about you? It doesn't even help much if you know that these figures are:

- the times in minutes it took a fire brigade to arrive at the fire, or
- the weight in grams of single portion packs of jam, or
- the number of rings before a phone was answered, or
- the minutes a bus was late after its scheduled arrival time.

As we discussed earlier in this chapter, variation is undesirable because it makes for unpredictability, and customers will seek to avoid suppliers whose output of services or goods are subject to high variation.

Imagine yourself as a manager in charge of one of the situations described above, sitting at your desk studying the table of figures. You know you must control variation. What you need is to derive information from this raw data, to help you decide whether the figures are acceptable or whether you should take some kind of action.

There are three types of summarizing measure which you might find useful:

- A single typical figure – the average or mean as it should be called, or the most frequently occurring figure. You could then compare this directly with the planned schedule or target, or specification. There is usually room for improvement. The average of these figures works out at 8.85.
- A single figure measure of spread. The range is the simplest and can be found easily by subtracting the smallest from the largest figure. The range in this case is fourteen. But the range is not the best measure of spread because it is derived from just two freak figures, which is not a reliable way to describe a large body of data! As you might expect, statisticians have developed better ways to measure the spread, or variability of a set of figures. The most important of these is the standard deviation, which we will look at in more detail later. Its value in this case is 3.13. The standard deviation is always smaller than the range – usually between a quarter and a sixth of the range. It is often represented by the Greek symbol sigma, σ.
- A profile of the spread of figures. Do most of the figures cluster tightly around the average with the numbers tailing off rapidly further away? (See Figure 3.21). Or are the figures spread uniformly across the range as in Figure 3.22? In fact the distribution is roughly bell-shaped. Bar charts or histograms of the figures are ways of helping you picture exactly what is going on. Their shape can often give you important clues on what to do to improve control.

As you know by now, if your data is in digital form on disk, your computer can produce bar charts quickly and easily. Lotus 1-2-3, can also display the average and standard deviation. The commands are as follows. For a block of figures extending from cell A2 to cell E6 on the spreadsheet, the command to display the average is @AVG(A2..E6) and to display the standard deviation it is @STD(A2..E6).

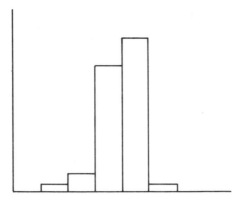

Figure 3.21   *Tightly clustered figures*

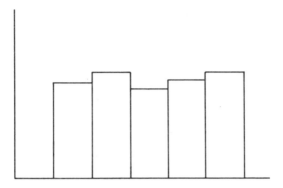

Figure 3.22   *Uniformly spread figures*

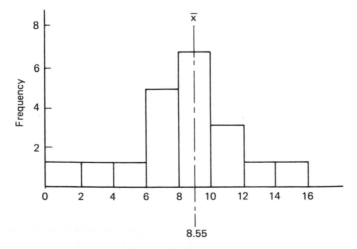

Figure 3.23   *Histogram of figures*

Alternatively if you have a pocket calculator which can be switched to statistical or SD mode, you can key in the list of figures one after another (your user manual will describe the exact procedure), and then just press the $\bar{x}$, x-bar key for the average to be displayed, and the σ, sigma key for the standard deviation to be displayed.

For decision-making, many managers feel more comfortable with just a graphical presentation, from which they can get a feel for the most commonly occurring figure, the amount and the type of spread of the figures. The table of figures we started with makes much more sense to most managers when displayed as in Figure 3.23. However, the single figure measures of average and standard deviation are still useful because they are more suitable for monitoring over time, to see if trends are in the right direction.

How to draw a frequency histogram

Some detail is lost when you summarize data in the form of a frequency histogram. This is because we group together values of about the same size in standard sized 'class intervals', and count how many readings there are in each class. This is how we get the hump-shaped profile with the hump showing that most values lie close to the average. If we counted the original values, it could quite easily happen that every value would be different. There could be no hump shape then, just a region on the x-axis where the values would be more densely packed.

To get a meaningful histogram, it is important that you choose the most appropriate size for the class interval. Choose intervals which are too many and too small, and you get a histogram with lots of superfluous peaks and troughs – misleading because they are the product of random chance and unlikely to have any meaning. But choose too few and too large a class interval, and although you can still see the main features of the distribution, you lose too much detail and will be in danger of missing real secondary features.

As a general rule, choose a class interval which will result in a total of between four and eight classes across the full range of values. A table of values that we can use as an example is shown in Table 3.1. They represent the mileages claimed by sales representatives over a period of weeks.

Table 3.1

552	747	478	602	404	581	744	567
612	559	541	648	707	599	622	720
460	644	523	625	633	606	530	658
655	645	508	666	648	637	460	540
493	642	690	555	667	525	456	493
795	705	608	480	592	651	655	610
523	548	555	495	532	567	689	591
577	412	590	712	520	578	522	678

1 Search the table for the largest and smallest values. They are 404 and 795. The range is therefore 391 and this should be split into about eight classes, which will therefore have a width of 391/8 = about 49. A suitable class interval to try would therefore be fifty. Our x-axis should therefore extend from 400 to 800, divided up as follows: 400 to 449, 450 to 499, 500 to 549 and so on.

2 The next step is to count the number of values which fall into each of these classes. The easiest way to do this is to write down the class intervals and then, taking the readings from the table one by one, mark a tally against the appropriate class interval:

Table 3.2

Class	Tally
400–449	‖
450–499	卌 ‖
500–549	卌 卌 ‖
550–599	卌 卌 ‖‖
600–649	卌 卌 ‖‖‖
650–699	卌 ‖‖‖
700–749	卌 ‖
750–799	‖

3 Now count the tallies, write down the frequency for each class, and check that the total of frequencies matches the total number of values in the table. You might note that the shape of the tallies actually gives you a clue as to what the histogram will turn out to look like – it is like a histogram turned on its side.

Table 3.3

Class	Tally	Frequency
400–449	‖	2
450–499	卌 ‖	7
500–549	卌 卌 ‖	11
550–599	卌 卌 ‖‖‖	13
600–649	卌 卌 ‖‖‖	14
650–699	卌 ‖‖‖	9
700–749	卌 ‖	6
750–799	‖	2
Total		64

4 Now just draw the histogram or bar chart as before (Figure 3.24). Now you can judge the average value near enough for decision-making: it is the value of the peak of the histogram – about 600. If you work it out using your calculator and the original data the average comes to 596 to the nearest whole number.

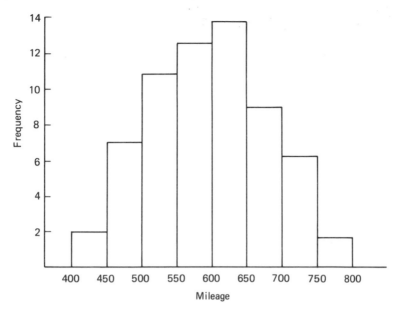

Figure 3.24 *Frequency histogram of mileages travelled by sales representatives*

Also the range is 800 − 400 = 400. A quarter of this is 100, and a sixth of this is sixty-seven, so we would expect the standard deviation to lie between these values. In fact working it out with your calculator it comes to eighty-six to the nearest whole number. But what is the standard deviation, and why is it superior to the range as a measure of scatter?

What is the standard deviation?

Like the range, it is a measure of the amount of scatter in a set of numbers. It is often represented by the Greek letter sigma, which looks like a number six which has fallen flat on its face, σ.

It is common in many distributions for most numbers to cluster around some central value which we call the mean. However, we also expect some numbers to be further away from the centre. We put this down to natural variation caused by many tiny influences, some negative and some positive, which on average tend to cancel each other out but occasionally stack up to produce a value further from the mean.

This effect results in the histogram having a humped shape, but if we only know the mean of a set of figures, we have no way of knowing whether the hump is low and wide, or high and narrow. For instance you must have seen boxes of matches with the label 'Average contents forty-eight matches'. This could be true if some boxes were empty and some had ninety-six matches in. In fact most boxes contain forty-eight and nearly all boxes have between forty-seven and forty-nine matches, but we have to take that on trust; the average figure on its own tells us nothing about how widely spread the distribution might be.

The range is unsatisfactory for describing the spread of a whole population of figures because it is derived from just two freak figures which in themselves are far from typical. It is a bit like using a giant and a dwarf to describe the population of a country. Also of course the range is unsatisfactory because if the giant or the dwarf died or left, the value of the range would suddenly change – perhaps by quite a large amount.

Remember as managers we really do need a satisfactory measure of scatter for monitoring in our efforts to reduce variation.

The standard deviation is a much more satisfactory measure of scatter because it is derived from every value in the set of figures. The word deviation is the clue: its calculation requires that we find out how far away each reading deviates from the mean. This is called the deviation of each reading. (See Figure 3.25.)

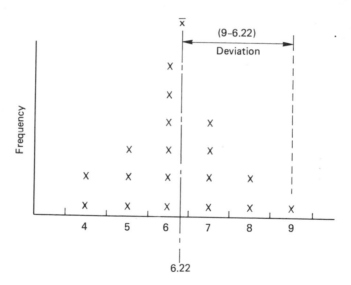

The largest figure, 9, deviates from the mean of 6.22 by 2.78.

Figure 3.25 *Deviation*

Then what? Well, we could find the average of all the deviations. This can be done, but there are some problems here. For instance if we just subtract the mean from each reading, we end up with about half the deviations negative for readings less than the mean, and half positive, for those greater than the mean. These then cancel each other out when we work out the average deviation; the answer always comes to zero, which is not much help.

Mathematically there are two ways round this problem. One is we could ignore the positive and negative signs and just work out the average size of the deviations. This is sometimes done and is called the Mean Absolute Deviation (MAD) but there is a better way.

You may remember from school that multiplying two negatives produces a positive. Well suppose we 'square' each of the positive and negative deviations – that is, multiply each by itself. We will then have a set of positive values for which we can calculate the average.

This mean squared deviation is more commonly known as the variance of the set of figures. But it too is not used much, mainly because it is so big and cannot be compared directly with the individual values from which it was derived. It is big because all the deviations were squared – remember? So what should we do? Unsquare it of course – that is, find the square root of the variance, or mean squared deviation. And that is exactly what the standard deviation is: the root of the mean squared deviations.

So now you know – and if you think the calculations sound tedious they certainly used to be before the calculator and the PC came galloping to the rescue. But it has always been valued because it plays a fundamental role in statistics and, of importance to managers, statistical process control (SPC). One example of SPC is the use of $\bar{x}$ charts and R charts which we will examine shortly, but first a word or two on the normal distribution.

What is a normal distribution?

The normal distribution is a particular bell-shaped distribution (Figure 3.26), similar in shape to the frequency distribution we produced earlier from the table of mileages claimed by sales representatives. If in

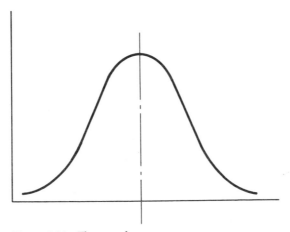

Figure 3.26 *The normal curve*

that example we had charted each value with a single point on the graph instead of a histogram bar, we could have drawn a curve through the points. It would have a similar bell shape to the one shown above, and we could say it approximated to the normal distribution.

In fact the normal curve has a formula defining the shape precisely, dependent on the mean and the standard deviation. Thus for a true normal curve, if we know the mean and the standard deviation, we know everything about that distribution. We know for instance that 95.45 per cent of all readings will lie within two standard deviations distance either side of the mean. (See Figure 3.27.)

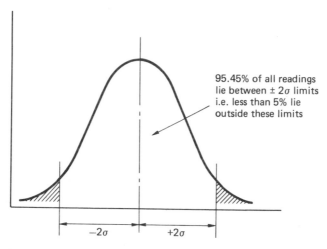

Figure 3.27   *The four-sigma limits*

This is very useful because if we have a process which we know produces a distribution approximately normal in shape, we can predict that about 95 per cent – that is about nineteen in every twenty – of all readings in the future will lie within plus and minus two sigma of the mean, so long as the process remains stable. Therefore if we get a reading outside these limits it is a warning sign. We should begin to suspect something might have gone wrong with our process. It is sufficiently unusual for it to happen just as a result of natural variation or common causes, for us to start thinking that perhaps there might be a single special cause which has upset the stability of the process to produce such a large deviation.

We also know that 99.8 per cent of all readings will lie within three standard deviations either side of the mean. These are the six-sigma limits used by IBM, Motorola and others (Figure 3.28).

Again they use them to help distinguish between common and special causes of variation. They are triggers for action because 998 in 1000 readings should lie within these limits. For a stable process the chances of a reading falling outside these limits due to expected or

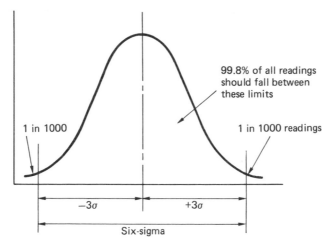

99.8% of all readings
should fall between
these limits

1 in 1000

1 in 1000 readings

−3σ

+3σ

Six-sigma

Figure 3.28 *Six-sigma*

common cause variation is about 1 in 1000 above, and 1 in 1000 below.

In other words, any reading outside the six-sigma limits is almost certainly due to a special cause. The process should be stopped and the cause discovered and eliminated to bring it back in control again.

So, with the normal distribution and the standard deviation, we have the makings of a system for monitoring processes to ensure that they continue to produce within specified limits, or at least to the best they are capable of. Let us now examine how such a system can work.

X-bar and R charts

These are a proven method of monitoring and controlling a manu-facturing process without the need for 100 per cent inspection.

Statistical process control has been around for fifty years or more. It was during the 1940s that Walter Shewhart, an American statistician, developed the control charts which are still in use today. I can only speculate as to how his thought processes evolved as he developed his charts, but his thinking probably went through the following phases.

To start with, he was obviously aware of the normal distribution, its standard deviation and the chances of values lying outside the four-sigma and six-sigma limits.

He also knew that inspection was expensive, and 100 per cent inspection adds quite a lot to the cost of each product without adding any extra value. And also as a statistician he would know that it is possible to infer conclusions about a whole population based upon what you find in a sample taken from that population.

He therefore probably started thinking about the process rather than the product, and whether it might be possible to control that by sampling rather than using 100 per cent inspection to weed out the out-of-specification products.

But he must also have been aware of a major difficulty, namely this. A process producing 5 per cent defective items is quite unacceptable, but is still difficult to detect by taking a single sample reading. The chance of detecting it will also be 5 per cent or a one in twenty chance each time. In fact we can work out that on average you would have to take about fifteen samples before you would have an evens chance of picking up a defective item.

On the credit side however, he would know that trends are useful in detecting and predicting change, and probably used a 'run chart' to show the output in comparison with the specification limits, and reveal trends as a sign of change in a process. (See Figure 3.29.)

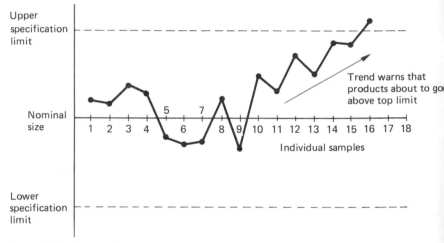

Figure 3.29 *The run chart*

A run chart is just a continuous graph for monitoring single samples taken from the output of the process. If there is any drift or gradual change taking place then this will eventually begin to show up as a trend on the graph.

But the masterstroke was when he tried taking small samples of five and averaging the readings, then charting the averages on a continuous graph, instead of the individual values. The sensitivity of the technique was amplified at least twentyfold, making it very likely that an output containing only 5 per cent defective items would be detected with the very first sample of five.

So how does it work? Well, there are two effects of averaging.

One effect is the random variations we expect from the process tend to be smoothed out in the averaging process. For instance, any value which is much larger than most of the output will be averaged along with four other less extreme values. Smoothing the results like this will reveal any underlying trends which might otherwise be obscured by the variation. (See Figure 3.30.)

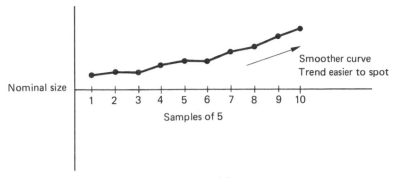

Figure 3.30   *Charting averages of samples of five*

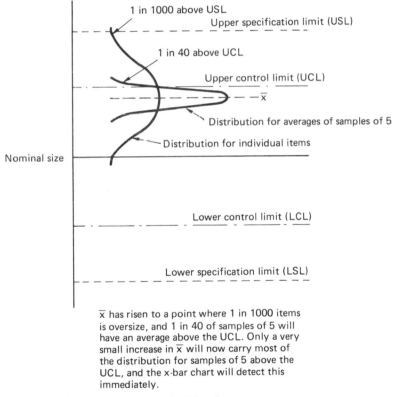

x̄ has risen to a point where 1 in 1000 items
is oversize, and 1 in 40 of samples of 5 will
have an average above the UCL. Only a very
small increase in x̄ will now carry most of
the distribution for samples of 5 above the
UCL, and the x-bar chart will detect this
immediately.

Figure 3.31   *Control limits and the X-bar chart*

Another effect is that a distribution of the averages will be a normal
distribution with very steep sides. If we draw in the four-sigma limits
for the average, we can see that only a very small change in the value
of the average, x̄, can then carry the majority of the distribution outside
of the limit, indicating a very good chance that the first sample of five
will have an average outside the limits, flagging a probable disturb-
ance to the process. These four-sigma limits for the average, x̄, are
called control limits, and are distinct from the specification limits
which will be more widely set (Figure 3.31).

Don't worry if this short explanation goes over your head. The important thing to remember is that averaging samples of five and using control limits instead of specification limits amplifies the sensitivity of the monitoring process by at least twentyfold. This makes the $\bar{x}$ chart very likely to detect an out-of-spec process at the first sample, even if it is only producing 5 per cent defective items.

Before we leave the theory to see how these charts work in practice, there is a last point to cover. By averaging samples of five, we have introduced a new problem. There is a small chance that our process may be disturbed in such a way that it starts to produce a wider scatter of results spread either side of the same average figure. For instance, if we are monitoring a filling process for filling jars to a certain weight, the process could become more erratic, producing some jars very much overweight and some very much underweight, but in a balanced way such that the average is not affected. Our $\bar{x}$-chart will not pick this up of course, because it is only sensitive to changes in the average.

However it is a simple matter to guard against this possibility. We produce a second chart called an R-chart for monitoring sample range. So on taking a sample of five, we must calculate the sample average, $\bar{x}$, and plot it on the $\bar{x}$-chart, and at the same time we must calculate the sample range, R, and plot it on the R-chart. The R chart has a control limit marked on it which is separate from and smaller than the overall allowable range in the whole output of the process. You would probably expect this to be the case, because the range within a sample will be smaller than the range within the overall output. After all, it would be extremely unlikely that the overall largest and overall smallest items should both be picked up within the same small sample of five.

The method of establishing the positions of the control limits on the control charts is beyond the scope of this introduction. It is however perfectly straightforward, and tables of factors are available to avoid the need to work out the values from first principles each time.

So let's now see how the charts are used in practice.

How to save money with X-bar charts

Let us start by taking a look at the economics of these charts. Is it worth getting into all this statistics? I hope by now you are convinced of how important it is to reduce variation, even though the major benefits are impossible to cost-justify. But aside from that, there can also be very large and immediate direct savings to be made, by cutting down on waste.

Some time ago I used to work as a packaging engineer for General Foods, an American company now known as Kraft General Foods. One of their lines was Maxwell House instant coffee which they packed in jars on automatic filling lines running at the rate of 400 jars per minute. They employed an operator who took five jars from the line every so

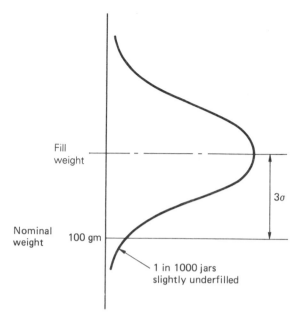

Figure 3.32 *Avoiding underfilling*

often, weighed the contents and plotted the results on x̄- and R-charts. We can do a few rough calculations now using estimated figures which cannot be too wide of the mark, to see if it was worth it.

How much does a 100 g jar of instant coffee retail for? Let us say £1.50, a nice round figure for the purposes of calculation. You can check in your cupboard or on the supermarket shelf: it is about right. So the coffee retails at 1.5 pence per gram.

Now General Foods must be sure of putting at least 100 g of coffee in each jar, or they will get on the wrong side of the Weights and Measures people, so they set their filling machines to an average fill weight of slightly greater than 100 g. Then, there will be very little chance of any underfilling due to the natural variation in fill weight produced by the filler. Ideally the filler should be set to fill at an average fill weight of just three-sigma above the nominal fill weight as in Figure 3.32.

In theory this will result in about one jar in a thousand being very slightly underfilled which in practice is as good as can be expected. To achieve a consistent average fill weight at this setting however, requires constant monitoring using control charts as outlined above.

Now suppose this approach saves on average just one gram of instant coffee per jar – far less than a teaspoon full – just a few grains on the end of your spoon. How much money will be saved in a year?

● 400 jars per minute over an eight hour shift is 400 × 60 × 8 = 192,000 jars.

- Over 5 days a week for a year this grows to 192,000 × 5 × 50 = 48,000,000 jars.
- The retail value of this in pounds is £48,000,000 × 1.5/100 = £720,000.

Now let us take just one-tenth part of this as the true figure, to take account of the retail mark-up, and lost production due to breakdowns and market restrictions. £72,000 would be enough to pay for the running of the control charts and still leave a saving of £1000 per week. Not bad, eh? – and that's just on one of many packing lines in the factory. It's amazing how those few grains from each jar add up, isn't it.

The charts have to be set up in advance by someone with the know-how to do it. Then anyone can fill in the charts and know what to do if the charts flag a warning. These are the steps:

1 Run the process for a while until it settles down. Then take about ten samples of five, making fifty in all. Calculate the averages and ranges of these samples and then look up in the appropriate tables for the positions of the control limits to set on the charts.

2 Now give the charts to the operators and tell them how often to take samples. This will depend on the value of the product, the rate of production, and the costs of sampling. If a sample shows the process has gone out of control, then all the output since the previous sample may have to be re-processed. The sampling should therefore be fairly frequent. But if the sampling involves the destruction of the product, then sampling should not be too frequent.

3 The operators should then take samples at the recommended intervals and if the $\bar{x}$ and the R plot satisfactorily within the control limits, they should allow the process to continue without adjustment.

4 If however an $\bar{x}$ value falls outside the two-sigma limits, this is a warning that the process may have gone out of control or is on the point of going out of control. However, even when the process is in control, the two-sigma limits will still only contain nineteen out of every twenty values, and one in forty readings should be expected to fall above the limit, and one in forty below. The rule is therefore that if there is no trend leading up to the out-of-limit value, the process should be allowed to continue without adjustment, but another sample of five should be taken immediately.

5 If this too falls outside the limit, the process should be stopped and reset, because with the process still in control, the chance of two out-of-limit values occurring consecutively is 1/40 × 1/40 or one in sixteen hundred. This is such a remote chance, that we must conclude that normal variation is not the cause and there is some other special cause for the two out-of-limit values which must be determined and eliminated to bring the process back into control.

I hope you can see now that control charts are a very powerful way of distinguishing between common and special causes of variation. If you are ever in charge of a process which you think may benefit from their application, you can find out more about them from the references that follow shortly.

Competence self-assessment

We have covered a lot of ground in this chapter. We touched on a variety of different techniques – all of direct relevance to managers – which are easy enough to read about, but it is not until you try using them yourself that you discover whether you truly understand how to use them.

If there are some of these techniques you haven't used before, try the following exercises. You can do some of them manually or using a PC, which ever you prefer. Either way, it can only add to your confidence and repertoire of management skills.

Pie charts and bar charts

1 Draw a pie chart to represent the data below, derived from the 1992 Microsoft/BIM survey of UK managers.

Table 3.4

Importance of IT to job	*Percentage*
Fundamental to your job	34
Important to your job	41
Supports job in the background	19
Largely peripheral to your job	4
Don't know	2
	100

When asked how important information technology is to their jobs, managers responded as shown in Table 3.4.

2 Recent mortality statistics produced for Oxfordshire Health Authority analysed causes of death under ninety different headings. In summary, there were 4681 deaths, of which 1255 were caused by neoplasm; 2134 were caused by circulation diseases; and the rest by a variety of other causes.

Show this data as a pie chart, and add a suitable title

3 In the 1992 Microsoft/BIM survey, British managers when asked what types of job they used information technology for, responded as shown in Table 3.5.

Table 3.5

Type of job	Percentage
Producing documents	53
Planning/forecasting/budgeting	46
Monitoring/reviewing performance	44
Communicating with others	14
Other jobs	3

Represent this data as a bar chart, suitably annotated and titled.

4 In their consolidated balance sheet at 30 June 1991, Amstrad plc reported current assets as follows:

Stocks	£175,928
Debtors	£112,987
Cash at bank and in hand	£69,805
	£358,720

Show this as a bar chart. Show it also as a pie chart. Which do you think is the most effective as a communication?

Scatter diagrams

5 Plot a scatter diagram for the following small (too small to be representative) sample, to see if there is any relationship between price and maximum speed in small cars. The data have been derived from *What Car?* magazine, August 1991. See Table 3.6.

Table 3.6

Model	Price (£)	Max Speed (mph)
Alfa Romeo 33 1.5 IE	10,415	113
BMW 316i	14,250	119
Fiat 126 BIS	3,296	72
Lada Riva 1300E	3,640	90
Nissan Micra 1.0 LS	5,717	91
Reliant Rialto	5,250	75
Renault Clio 1.2 RL	7,350	96
Rover Mini City	5,262	84
Toyota Starlet 1.0 GL	8,450	89

Number the cars one to nine and mark each point on the graph with the appropriate reference number.

6 Texmills DIY wants to see if sales are boosted by newspaper advertising. The level of advertising, and the volume of sales for each of seven months are shown in Table 3.7.

Table 3.7

Month	Advertising spend (£)	Sales volume (£)
June	8,630	102,430
July	4,480	103,720
August	19,110	151,220
September	12,160	148,990
October	3,910	53,100
November	8,470	68,800
December	17,140	118,750

Chart this data as a scatter diagram. What does it indicate?

Pareto analysis

7 The stores in a hospital department holds just ten items in stock. The usage and values of the items are shown in Table 8.

Calculate the value of annual usage for each item. Rank them in descending order, and plot them as a Pareto curve.

Table 3.8

Item	Annual usage (items)	Unit value (£)
1	244	68.10
2	585	58.30
3	76	76.35
4	74	52.64
5	7,413	4.60
6	63,800	3.21
7	2,135	2.95
8	558	4.30
9	424	9.20
10	468	13.45

Which approximately 20 per cent of the items form approximately 80 per cent of the annual usage value?

Which items would you classify as A, B and C items?

8   There are twelve products in the range offered by a marketing
     company. The sales revenue attributable to each product is shown in
     Table 3.9.

Table 3.9

Product reference	Sales revenue (£000)
1	310
2	140
3	44
4	180
5	86
6	1,067
7	116
8	96
9	68
10	720

Set these products on a Pareto curve, and thus identify the few vital
products from amongst the many other important products.

Cause-effect diagrams

9   An airline operating out of Heathrow has a problem of late flight
     departures. A quality group is convened to uncover the causes of late
     departure. During a meeting of the group, the main reasons suggested
     by members were as follows:

- Aircraft arrival delayed.
- Cockpit crew late or unavailable.
- Aircraft problem requiring maintenance.
- Late on-board catering supplies.
- Slow security clearance procedures.
- Pushback tug unavailable when required.
- Baggage handlers late to aircraft.
- Fuel late to aircraft.
- Air traffic control delays.
- Cabin cleaners late.
- Delays due to bad weather.
- Flight weight and balance sheet late.
- Delay for late passengers.
- Cabin crews late.

Prepare a cause-effect (Ishikawa) diagram with bones for the 4Ms
and 'Other' causes. Fill in the effect on the right hand side, then attach
the causes listed above to the appropriate bones.

10 Write down in two or three words a problem or undesirable effect you are aware of at work. Construct a fishbone diagram consisting of the 4Ms and any other bones necessary, and then attach possible causes to the appropriate bones. If possible, discuss the diagram with someone else familiar with the problem, and see if together you can add to the possible causes.

Histograms

11 A fruit farmer harvests cooking apples from his trees. The weights of apples in kilograms yielded by each of thirty trees are shown in Table 3.10.

Table 3.10

41.3	52.6	58.9	49.3	53.6
66.8	46.3	51.3	54.4	65.1
45.8	62.3	42.3	46.8	48.8
48.7	51.7	48.3	56.2	53.2
54.1	64.7	63.8	47.2	64.6
46.1	57.5	49.4	65.2	59.3

Produce a frequency histogram of this data, using a class interval of five kilograms.

From the histogram, estimate the average weight of apples produced per tree. Compare this value with the true mean of the above figures, computed using your PC or calculator.

Divide the range by four. This should give you a rough estimate of the standard deviation. Compute the standard deviation using your calculator or PC, from the table of figures above. How does it compare with the estimate?

Would you say the histogram has a shape which approximates to the Normal curve?

12 A company makes drinking chocolate as a powder to be made up with hot milk. The company packs it for sale in containers marked 250 g. The filler delivers a measured volume of the powder, which because of variations in the density of the powder results in a small amount of variation in fill weight. The contents of one thousand successive packs were weighed, and the results are shown in Table 3.11.

Produce a frequency histogram of these figures. Draw in the nominal container weight. Estimate the average fill weight being produced by the filler. Should the filler be adjusted to another average fill weight?

Table 3.11

Weight (g)	Frequency
Over 250.0, up to 250.5	5
Over 250.5, up to 251.0	17
Over 251.0, up to 251.5	44
Over 251.5, up to 252.0	92
Over 252.0, up to 252.5	150
Over 252.5, up to 253.0	192
Over 253.0, up to 253.5	192
Over 253.5, up to 254.0	150
Over 254.0, up to 254.5	92
Over 254.5, up to 255.0	44
Over 255.0, up to 255.5	17
Over 255.5, up to 256.0	5

Does this histogram approximate in shape to the Normal curve? If so, why might this be worth knowing?

References and further reading

Caplen, R. H. (1988). *A Practical Approach to Quality Control*. Hutchinson.
Curwin, J. and Slater, R. (1991). *Quantitative Methods for Business Decisions* (3rd edn). Chapman and Hall.

4 Computers, programs and communications

Why is this chapter relevant?

Computers are business machines: they are as relevant now as the telephone and the typewriter were when they were first introduced during the era of the carrier pigeon. There is a difference though. Computers are much more complex machines. Unlike typewriters and phones it is not immediately obvious how they work.

Does this matter? To draw another comparison you don't need to know what goes on under the bonnet when you drive your car to the supermarket or pick up the kids from school. But professional users must know more about their machines than casual users. You can be sure that Nigel Mansell knows quite a lot about engines, gearboxes, differentials and brake systems. Such knowledge can be crucial, especially in a competitive environment.

Computers are changing our jobs as managers:

- We can use them to communicate more freely as we reach out through networks to find the information we need.
- We can make better decisions because we understand situations better through modelling and 'what-if' analysis.
- We can store virtually unlimited numbers of files – and find any one of them in seconds.

Professional users need to know more than just how to drive their machines: when the going gets tough, those that do will come through in better shape.

Microsoft/IM survey results

The headline in Figure 4.1 appeared on the front page of *Management News*, the newspaper of the Institute of Management (IM), in March 1992. So you are not the only one with a guilty secret! The figures quoted in the article come from a survey of IM members carried out jointly by MicroSoft and IM. The results show what managers think about computers:

Computers are already important in most managers' jobs.
- Seventy-six per cent have direct use of screens and keyboards.

Management News

No. 84 MARCH, 1992   THE NEWSPAPER OF THE BRITISH INSTITUTE OF MANAGEMENT

Crucial stage approaching in merger moves

THE merger of BIM with the Institution of Industrial Managers is reaching a crucial stage.

Later this month IIM members will be voting on the merger, while BIM members will vote at a special EGM to be held at 5 pm on April 30 at the Strand Palace Hotel, London.

A joint prospectus which sets out the merger proposals in detail has been drawn up by both institutes and copies are being mailed to all members with this issue of *Management News*.

Both IIM and BIM are confident the merger will proceed successfully.

BIM chairman, Sir Derek Hornby said: "We have made great progress towards bringing our two institutes closer together. The existing affiliation agreement between us and the IIM has worked well in the past but now it is time for us to forge even closer links.

"As a new merged institute we will bring together the strengths of the separate elements. Our representational work on behalf of IIM and BIM is outstanding. Our certificate and diploma programmes are among the best in the country and the Management Information Centre is the largest of its kind in Europe.

"Our strengths will be reinforced by the merger with IIM."

Sir Derek added: "IIM is bringing its extremely successful leader series into the new institute and this will enable a whole new sector of management to benefit from this unique educational resource.

"Our future lies in the new larger combined Institute of Management and I urge everyone to vote in favour of the proposals."

BIM has undertaken a major communications exercise to ensure all members appreciate the benefits of the new institute. The director general, chairman and senior council members are touring the country in an effort to meet individual members at first hand. In addition a comprehensive slide presentation has been made available to branches.

● Anyone who has not received a copy of the prospectus should contact Valerie Hamill on 071-497 0580.

Survey reveals 92 per cent 'uncomfortable' with hi-tech

Managers scared of computers

BRITAIN'S managers are scared of computers. More than 75 per cent say they use computers directly in their work, and a third feel they could not do their job without them.

But 92 per cent admit they are uncomfortable with the technology.

Figure 4.1 *Management News headline*

- Seventy-five per cent rate information technology (IT) as fundamental or important to their jobs.
- Forty per cent of managers under age forty couldn't do their job without IT.
- Thirty-four per cent of all managers couldn't do their jobs without IT.

So how should we interpret these figures? About threequarters of managers actually use computers, but nearly all (92 per cent) feel uncomfortable with the technology! The survey suggests that managers are not adequately trained in the technology. Computers are not easy to use properly (though they are getting easier) and few managers feel they get adequate time, training and support to develop the necessary skills. Most are left to pick up what they can from colleagues at work.

And what do you make of the difference between managers over and under age forty? Is it because schools have only recently been able to afford computers? Few managers over forty came across computers while at school or college, whereas many under forty will have done. There may be another reason too: managers over forty will tend to be in more senior posts, doing jobs where it is less obvious how computers can be advantageous.

Computers are likely to get more important to most managers' jobs in the future:
- Ninety-seven per cent feel IT will have a significant impact on their work in the future.
- Seventy-one per cent expect changes in how work is organized, involving new management processes and teamworking.
- Over half (54 per cent) expected home and teleworking to form part of the future pattern, with managers remote from each other collaborating electronically on computers, seeing identical screens and working with the same shared data.
- One-third of managers expected IT to have a flattening effect on the organization chart, reducing the layers in the hierarchy and simplifying the flow of information.

Computers can deliver important advantages:
- Ninety-four per cent believe computers can improve performance.
- Eighty-five per cent believe computers can improve quality and service.
- Sixty per cent believe computers can save them money.

Clearly managers don't need persuading of the importance of computers to their jobs – and yet 92 per cent are uncomfortable with them. You won't therefore be surprised to learn managers feel that –

Computers are not used as well as they could be:
- Only 6 per cent believe IT is being used to its full potential in their organization.

- Only 9 per cent use computers to share information with their colleagues.
- Fifty-three per cent use PCs most frequently as glorified typewriters to produce documents.

Survey conclusions

These results paint a rather disturbing picture. You can read a fuller account of the survey in *Management Today*, February 1992 issue, but the main observations are as follows:

- Most managers use PCs mainly to edit documents – an inappropriate use of senior management time.
- Few managers use PCs for monitoring customers or competitors.
- Few managers are linked into networks for sharing information and teamworking.

And the reasons managers quote for not applying computers in more imaginative ways? The main ones quoted are:

- Time it takes to master systems.
- Lack of training and technical support.
- Use of jargon.

I expect these conclusions ring a few bells for you too, but clearly they are oversimplified. If managers believed their promotion prospects depended on how widely and imaginatively they used computers they would take the time, get the training, insist on the technical support and learn the jargon. Does your chief executive say 'Get your report printed and circulated by Friday and we'll discuss it at next week's meeting'? Or does she/he say 'Circulate your report on the network, arrange an e-mail conference and we'll decide by Friday'? As with most things, we all take our lead from the chief executive – often a technophobe – and hence our reluctance to change. The paperless office is not yet with us, though it seems we are headed that way at the moment.

One problem holding us back is that it is difficult to work with, and feel you 'own' your copy of a report on screen. For instance, you can't easily highlight passages, make notes in the margin, or compare two pages at the same time. So printer makers needn't worry – we're always going to need print-outs for our own records though paperwork for circulation seems destined to decline. Cumbersome printing and manual postal delivery just won't be fast enough soon. The accelerating pace of business means that to keep up, easy access to immediate information is becoming essential.

Jargon

Managers claim that the jargon makes it difficult to learn about computers, and you probably understand why. Have you ever felt excluded from discussion and vaguely guilty because you don't know for instance what RAM is, or resentful even, because you suspect the computer people are exploiting the situation? But all specialists use jargon, and computer people are no worse than accountants with their internal rates of return and quick ratios.

Jargon performs a useful function, making it much easier for those in the know to discuss difficult, but commonly occurring concepts. Take the word 'offside' in football for instance. Think how difficult it would be for a radio sports commentator if forbidden to use the word offside for fear of excluding some listeners. Or ask a lawyer what a 'contract' is, and you'll be treated to a short lecture. Every professional or special interest group has its own jargon and you can probably think of examples in photography, motor sport, knitting and hi-fi, as well as computers. Magazines serving these special interests often have a beginners' page devoted to explaining week by week different jargon terms – a kind of extended glossary. Magazine publishers know that jargon can exclude newcomers, but it can also act as a pointer to areas of knowledge which newcomers need to acquire if they are to understand reports or join in any meaningful debate on the subject. So in the best popular magazine tradition, let us also start by busting five key jargon terms:

● Hardware
● Software
● Memory
● Printouts
● Networks

Hardware

If it is part of a computer system and you can switch it on, it is hardware. Hardware forms part of most business information systems, and when you use it, you and the hardware together form the human-computer interface, across which data and information is exchanged. You can add information to the system using an input device – usually a keyboard – and you can receive information from the system as a display on a screen, or a print-out from a printer. These are the usual computer output devices.

Business information systems usually consist of a number of computers all linked together to form a communications network, with information able to flow through the network from one computer to another. If you work in an organization which has such a system, then the computer on your desk can be thought of as a sub-system, just part of the whole information system.

What is a system? All systems have inputs, storage, processes and outputs. For instance your hot water system at home has cold water and fuel as the main inputs. The heating of the water in the boiler is the process, and the hot water may be stored in the cylinder before being drawn off as output in the bathroom and kitchen.

Similarly a business information system has inputs of data which can be stored in various ways before being processed into information which can be drawn off by users wherever it is needed. The same is true of the subsystem – the computer on your desk. It too has inputs, storage, processes and outputs.

We are getting deep into jargon country with output devices alone quite capable of filling several pages with technical terms. We will return to these later and move on now to software.

Software

In contrast to hardware which is solid and permanent, software consists of programs or lists of instructions for the computer to carry out. Like telephone messages they are intangible and impermanent, and can be sent via cables, telephone lines and satellite transmissions. Software exists as binary code, a series of pulses switching on and off – rather like the dots and dashes of morse code, to which computers can respond.

A computer program starts its life by being typed by a programmer into a computer as a set of instructions called a file. Each file is designed to get the computer to perform a particular function, and when first typed in, exists only in the computer's main memory circuits and would be lost if the computer were switched off. Programmers therefore take copies of their work by recording each new file onto a disk which can be played back if necessary, to re-load the program into the computer. The disks are made of magnetic material rather like that used for audio and video tapes, and the code is saved as a series of microscopic magnetized spots and spaces. There is much more to learn about software but in this brief introduction we have now reached an appropriate point to turn to the next jargon term.

Memory

If you have ever heard computer buffs talking about Kay and Meg, don't get the wrong idea. They are not talking about two women in the Computer Department – they are just referring to the amount of memory a computer has. 500kb (pronounced 500 'kay') means 500 kilobytes, and 2Mb (pronounced 2 'meg') means two megabytes. Kilo means one thousand, and mega means one million, so 500kb is the same as half a megabyte.

So what is a byte? Simple – a byte is eight bits. And a bit? This is a contraction of the term binary digit, which exists as the presence (or absence) of a magnetized spot on a disk, or the presence (or absence) of a signal pulse travelling down a wire. Up to eight bits are needed to code each of the fifty-two alphabetic characters (including upper and lower case), the ten numeric characters, and the other punctuation and special characters used by computers. So the number of bytes of memory is the number of characters that can be stored. Typically a single page of text from a report may take up about 2kb of space in the main memory of a computer. Main memory is usually referred to as RAM, standing for random access memory, because the computer can go straight to any part of a file without having to search from the beginning – as would be the case if the file had been recorded onto tape. The amount of RAM a computer has is an important indicator of its power and capacity – rather like engine size in cars. There are many other forms of storage which we will return to later.

Printouts

Computer printouts can be that concertina-fold paper with the holes down the side and green horizontal stripes which make your eyes glaze over – or it can be crisp white pages with clear diagrams and elegant text that looks just like it has been typeset.

Until recently most computer printers used to be direct descendants of the typewriter, striking metal characters one after the other through an inked ribbon onto the paper, and printing a line of text at a time. The expansion in the use of PCs however brought a demand for cheaper printers – including ones which could handle images as well as text. The dot matrix printer became very popular, capable of producing a wide range of different alphanumeric characters, and images too. Instead of using many different metal characters, the dot matrix uses a single print head and builds up characters and images from dots created by needles struck through an inked ribbon. A typical print head has twenty-four needles arranged in a six by four rectangle, from which each character can be constructed. For instance, a simple capital 'L' would only require the needles in the bottom row and left column. (See Figure 4.2.)

Images can also be constructed by 'bit-mapping', producing a black and white picture from thousands of dots. The picture is broken down into columns and rows of tiny picture cells or pixels, and the needles

Figure 4.2   *A dot-matrix letter 'L'*

in the print head are fired by bits of data in one of the two binary states, fed to the printer by the computer.

Dot matrix printers are cheap and versatile, but they are noisy and the print quality is often poor (draft quality), though quite good results can be achieved by changing the ribbon regularly and getting the printer to strike more than once over each line of text (near-letter quality, or NLQ).

Daisy wheel printers can handle text only but produce letter quality. Each character is held on a separate petal of the daisy wheel, and a new character-set, or new typeface can easily be selected just by changing the daisy wheel. Again they are very noisy and in a busy office they need to be put in a sound-proofed cabinet.

The latest types of printer are the ink-jet and the laser. The ink-jet works on the same principle as the dot matrix, but instead of needles, fires microscopic jets of ink onto the paper to produce the bit-mapped characters and images. The laser on the other hand owes more to the photocopier than the typewriter. A needle-sharp laser beam scans the surface of a printing drum to create a pattern of electrostatic charge. Toner powder is attracted to the charged areas, then transferred to the paper and melted on. Laser printers are more expensive but are fast and produce excellent quality. Ink-jets are cheaper but still produce very good results. Both types of printer are quiet in use.

Printed output is often referred to as hard copy output because, like hardware, it is fixed and difficult to change. Other forms of output are much easier to change, edit and develop. For instance output to disk, or through a network.

Networks

For instance, suppose your secretary has typed your report and you need to check it through. They could print a draft copy and pass it to you for marking up. Then you could pass it back and they could edit the original on their disk before printing again. Should you check it again before it is replicated and circulated?

Alternatively the first draft produced by your secretary could be transferred electronically to your screen by exchanging disks, or better still through a network connection. You could scan through it making corrections on screen as you go, then send the edited version back to your secretary's computer for her to print, replicate and circulate.

Networks – great for teamworking like this – come in two forms. LANs or local area networks serve a single site, often a single room. WANs or wide area networks can extend world-wide. LANs are fast, often using 'parallel' communications between computers, with eight or more wires so that the eight bits of a byte can all be sent down the network at the same time, each along its own wire. WANs however often use 'serial' connections, a single wire or a twisted pair carrying bits as pulses following each other one at a time down the same single wire.

Often it is impractical to have special lines laid just for the network, and some links may be established through the communications services of bulk carriers such as British Telecom, Mercury and others. Telephone networks though, are designed to carry voice messages and sounds, not the binary voltage pulses that computers use, and so a special piece of gear called a modem is used to convert the pulses into sounds when sending messages into the telephone network, and to convert sounds back again into computer code when receiving. Modem is short for modulator-demodulator, and its circuitry can be installed as a separate box between the computer and the telephone socket, or as a circuit board or 'card' mounted in one of the spare slots actually inside the PC main unit.

Automating routine jobs

So, hardware is the machinery and software is the lists of instructions which drive the machinery to automate routine office work. So far we have concentrated on the smaller computer known as the PC or personal computer, because they are so common nowadays, yet consist of the same components as the larger machines known as mainframes. We will leave the bigger computers until the next chapter. The PC is complicated enough to start with; it is so complex even expert users don't profess to know everything. No single person can know everything there is to know about how the PC works: the further you dig down into the detailed design the more specialized it becomes.

Fortunately though, you only need to learn a bit about the basics to develop an instinct for what should be possible. Then it just boils down to finding the commands to invoke the appropriate routines. Also as time goes by and computers develop, it is becoming more and more possible to use the PC without knowing anything about the workings. You can use the keyboard for inputs, the screen for output, and regard the system in between as a mysterious 'black box'. But occasionally to save time, or to avoid effort, you may want to try something out of the ordinary, such as copying data to a colleague or supplier and without knowing something about the workings you won't even know if it is possible. PCs are becoming fairly easy to use – like driving a car. But unusual situations can develop, and then the knowledgeable user is likely to come through in better shape.

Using software

There are three main reasons why managing information electronically is superior to manual methods:

- Speed of access: you can search with blinding speed in order to find particular facts or figures.
- Ease of editing: you can change information with supreme ease by adding, changing or deleting it.

● Ease of saving: you can copy and store information freely and instantly.

For instance you can take out a file, use it or change it, then put it back again fast and easily, even if you have many thousands of files.

This all probably sounds too general to strike much of a chord with you and so let us take a look at how these three processes of accessing, editing and saving actually work with real information and real software. Well, information comes in three main forms:

● Text or words
● Numbers and formulae
● Graphics or images

Different software packages are designed to handle each of these. For instance if you work with text, you should use word processing software, whereas for numbers you should perhaps choose a spreadsheet package. For graphics, computer-aided design software might be appropriate. Each of these types of package are excellent when working with the main form of information for which they were designed, but have only limited capacity for handling the other two forms, but the processes of accessing, editing and saving, work just the same whatever the software package and form of information being used.

Seeing as more word processing is done on PCs than any other task, let us use that to illustrate the principles. Then we can see how exactly the same principles apply in spreadsheets. And finally we will do a round-up of the other packages to see how the principles apply there too.

Word processing

All work produced on PCs is held in files. A file can be as short as a single line memo, or as long as the chapter of a book. The upper limit on size would eventually be restricted by the amount of RAM your PC has, but this is not likely to be a problem nowadays. Even fairly ancient PCs can handle hundred page documents, and most modern machines can handle a file size of a thousand pages or more. In fact most word processed files are just a few pages long, which at two or three kilobytes per page means most files are probably about two to ten kb in size.

Accessing

You can pull out and view a file in seconds using the PC by pressing a few keys, whereas manually it involves getting up from your desk and walking to the filing cabinets, finding the right drawer, thumbing across the names . . . Of course you need to know the file name and the ease of accessing a particular file depends in both cases on how the files are named and organized. We will discuss file organization later as it applies to all files, not just word processed files. But even if you don't know the name of the file you are seeking, you should still be able to find it fairly quickly. If you can think of any unique word which appears in the file you want, you can ask your PC to search all your files for that key word. The PC will then display a list of filenames, indicating which files if any, contain the key word.

Editing

This is the process which is so easy with a computer that it makes possible completely new ways of working with information. Information on paper is difficult to change. Consider for instance a sales letter produced on a conventional typewriter. Any typographical errors usually require the whole letter to be retyped, during which there is always the possibility that further typos will be introduced. With typewriter technology, perfection was difficult to achieve. It depended upon well-trained and conscientious secretarial staff.

The word processor has changed all that by making it possible to store electronically the sequence of key strokes made by the typist. The sequence is displayed on screen as it would appear on paper and any changes are simple to make. Words can be inserted or deleted and the text following the change moves across to accommodate the change. If there are then too many or too few words to fit on that line, words automatically roll over or back to just fill the line where the change was made, and all subsequent lines are adjusted as well. Then when you have got the sales letter appearing on screen just how you want it, you can print it.

If later you want a different version of the letter, printed between narrower margins, or in a different typeface, it is a piece of cake to do. No need to rekey all the words – the same long string of keystrokes stored in memory or on disk can simply be set to print in the new format. Also 'cut and paste' operations are simple to do electronically. Suppose you want to start the letter with a sentence which is in the middle of the letter at present. No problem. Mark the required block of text and indicate where you want it moving to and the computer will do the rest.

Also, in just the same way you can take a block of text from one file and insert it anywhere in another. This facility opens up new possibilities and accounts for the huge growth in junk mail we receive now. It makes possible for sales letters to be tailored to the circumstances of each reader. In the days of the typewriter, mailing shots used to be Xeroxed or printed, with the space for the name and address left blank for a typist to fill later. It was obvious to the reader and the letters also had to be couched in very general terms to cover a wide range of reader circumstances. The readers could see they were being batch processed. not very flattering and as a consequence not very effective as a sales pitch. Now with a word processor and a little ingenuity, the same process can be performed, but with results that look like they have been typed individually for each reader. The bulk of the letter can still be standard, with spaces left for the operator to fill in personal comments based on knowledge of the particular reader.

The direct mail organizations have developed this to a fine art now and it is fascinating to figure out how a particular mail shot has been generated. Often information from several different files must be used automatically by the computer – something more powerful than a PC! – to bring together in a single letter the main text, your name and address from a mailing list file, and perhaps the name and address of your nearest dealer from a dealer file.

Next time you get a mail shot from *Time-Life, Readers Digest* or a car maker, see if you can spot the joins between standard text and text tailored to your address. Direct mail is a specialized business relying more on automatic data processing than on conventional word processing. Word processing allows the operator to interact with the text on screen but this too requires several files of information to be available. Stuck for the right word to use? Type the nearest you can think of straight off, then invoke the thesaurus. Your PC will refer to the thesaurus file and display a dozen or more nearly equivalent words. Point to the word you want and the PC can automatically insert it in place of the word you first thought of. It can also find and replace all other occurrences of a particular word, wherever it occurs in a document.

Uncertain about the spelling of a word? Invoke the spell checker and your PC will refer to its dictionary file to check that a word, or every word in your document is a real word. It will spot 'beleive' and ask if you want to replace it with 'believe', but will pass over 'rain' even when you should have used 'reign'. PCs are not very good at interpreting context yet, but they are getting better. Programs are available which will check your writing style, which mostly do simple things like checking average word, sentence and paragraph length, but they can also spot split infinitives and long dependent clauses.

It is the simple things word processors do well, like finding and replacing a particular word, name, or string of characters. For instance in a long report appraising a computer project, you might wish to remove a jargon term and replace it with something more generally understandable. 'Find and replace' allows you to key in the string to be found, and also the string to replace it with. The computer can then find every occurrence of the jargon term, 'DCF return', say, and replace it with 'internal rate of return'. For a 10,000 word report which would take you an hour or more just to read, finding and replacing can be completed by your word processor in seconds.

Saving

If we wish to describe word processing in 'systems' terminology, then text entry at the keyboard is input, editing is the process, and printing is the output. It is the input stage, involving manual text entry which is the bottleneck; and that is why cheap storage on disk has been developed. Once the text has been entered, it can be processed, stored, accessed and printed with great ease and at lightning speed.

So as a general rule you should never just print a hard copy of a word processing session. Always save any work at the keyboard – either after entering original text, or after an editing session. Then you can avoid ever having to type out in full the same or similar text again. For all but the smallest of files it is easier and much cheaper to edit an old file stored on disk than it is to type it out again. The only exceptions are very short two or three line memos and the like, which may be cheaper to retype than to access from disk – especially if the disk space is cluttered up with thousands of other two or three liners.

When you save a new file you have to think of a suitable name for it, usually limited to a maximum of eight alphanumeric characters plus a three character extension after a full stop. There are however some characters and sequences you should avoid using in file names, as they can cause trouble. It depends on the operating system your computer uses, but you should avoid using sequences to which the operating system ascribes special meanings. For instance with MS-DOS, file names should never start with the three-letter strings CON AUX LST PRN and NUL followed by a space, as the computer may then mistake the filename for a special command.

Also, the extensions .COM .EXE .BAT and .SYS must never be used for normal word processor files because they are reserved for use by the computer in identifying program and operating system files. So as a simple rule to keep you out of trouble, avoid these four extensions, and avoid using spaces in your file names.

In this brief introduction to word processing we have seen how information in the form of text is accessed, edited and saved. Let us now turn to see how these processes are achieved with another form of information – numerical information.

Spreadsheets

The most popular software for handling numbers and graphs on PCs is the spreadsheet, which makes it possible to manipulate numbers and formulae in all the same ways that a word processor manipulates text. For instance you can insert and delete, copy or move blocks of numbers and so on, which is great for dealing with tables of figures, but if that was all a spreadsheet could do, you could manage almost as easily with your word processor.

The big extra advantage that spreadsheets offer is their ability to interpret numbers as values which, unlike words can be added, subtracted, displayed as a graph, sorted into order of value, averaged . . . that is, used in calculations to derive useful results for decision-making and control.

Entering data

When you switch on and first load the spreadsheet software package, you are presented with an empty screen – as happens with many word processors – only this time the screen is divided up into columns and rows – in some ways a bit like the squared paper we first used for arithmetic at primary school. Each column has an identifying letter A, B, C . . . etc. at the top, and each row is numbered, so that each square or 'cell' has its own address. For instance the first or 'home' cell at the top left of the screen where column A crosses row 1 is called A1. (See Figure 4.3.)

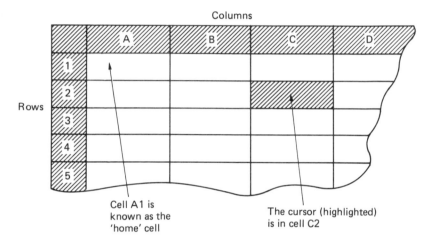

Figure 4.3 *An empty spreadsheet*

There are three different types of entry you can make in a cell:

● A label – alphanumeric characters.
● A value – numbers.
● A formula – e.g. (A2+A3).

It is this ability to enter formulae using cell addresses as variables that makes spreadsheets so wonderfully versatile. For instance the example above (A2+A3), entered in cell A1 would cause the sum of the values currently entered in cells A2 and A3 to be displayed in cell A1.

Also there is one other special type of formula you can use with spreadsheets, which will derive functions of values entered, such as:

● The average of a range of values.
● The standard deviation of a range of values.
● The logarithm of a value.

Modern spreadsheet packages hold a library of these special functions, making it possible for you to construct spreadsheet programs to perform quite sophisticated analysis of numerical data.

One example of analysis which is very commonly performed on a spreadsheet is cash-flow forecasting, which featured right at the beginning of this book in the opening scenario with the executive performing 'what-if' analysis and worrying about costs and margins.

Cash is very important. Running out of cash can bring an organization to its knees quicker than becoming loss-making or unprofitable. Without cash an organization cannot pay its employees and will cease to operate. That is why cash-flow forecasting is so useful: it analyses future income and expenditure month by month to check that on average there is a positive flow of cash into the organization, and that reserves are adequate to cover for any months when cash flow is expected to be negative.

Cash-flows are normally constructed for a year or more into the future, to calculate the effects on the current account of anticipated income and expenditure each month. We know we will receive bills in the future; we know their likely size and when they will arrive. We also

	A	B	C	D	E
1	Cash flow forecast: R. Ingmain, electrician				
2		January	February	March	Apr
3	Income:				
4	Sales	2570.00	2600.00	2650.00	
5	Repairs	140.00	150.00	160.00	
6	TOTAL INCOME	(B4 + B5)	(C4 + C5)	(D4 + D5)	
7	Expenses:				
8	Wages	1500.00	1500.00	1500.00	
9	Rent	200.00	200.00	200.00	
10	Phone	65.00			
11	TOTAL EXPENSE	(B8 + B9 + B10)	(C8 + C9 +C10)	(D8 + D9 + D10)	
12	Net cash flow	(B6 − B11)	(C6 − C11)	(D6 − D11)	
13	Opening balance	450.00	+B14	+C14	
14	Closing balance	(B13 + B12)	(C13 + C12)	(D13 + D12)	

NB When the formulae are typed in, the
spreadsheet computes and displays
the resulting values.

Figure 4.4 *Spreadsheet cash flow analysis*

know roughly how much revenue to expect from forecasted sales, and when it will be paid to us. So we allocate twelve columns of cells on the spreadsheet to the twelve months of the forecast period, one column for each month. Then in the first column for the first month, we make two lists, one for all the income we expect to receive, and another for all the expenses we must meet. By entering formulae at the foot of each list, we can get the spreadsheet to produce the totals of income and expense for the month.

We can also enter a formula to display the difference between income and expense, which is called the cash flow for the month. If income is greater than expense, the cash flow that month is positive, and if smaller, it is negative. The cash flow can then be used to adjust the balance of the current account at the end of that month, as shown in Figure 4.4.

So, our spreadsheet shows for the first month, say January, the total income, total expenditure, cash flow, and the balance of the current account at the beginning and end of the month. The balance at the end of January – called the closing balance for January – will of course be the opening balance for February. You can get the spreadsheet to carry the value forward by simply typing the address of the cell where it appeared before into the cell where you want it to appear again.

Once you have worked out the formulae you need and entered them into the January column of the spreadsheet, you can then copy them all across to the other eleven columns for a twelve month forecast. This can be done in just a few keystrokes.

The Copy command is just one of many commands available, which in Lotus 1-2-3 are arranged in the form of a hierarchy of menus. You invoke these commands by first typing the / key, which brings up the main menu at the top of the screen. You select an option from the menu by highlighting with the cursor, or by typing the initial letter of the option.

The cash flow forecast is a kind of financial model of your operations, and you can play with it assuming different favourable or unfavourable circumstances. For instance, what will happen if labour costs or interest rates go up? What effect will this have on your cash balance month by month? Will you have to negotiate an increase in your overdraft limit with the bank? When you play 'what-if' with your model in this way, you develop a feel for how sensitive your operations are, to an increase in interest rates for instance, and if necessary take action to reduce exposure to this risk.

Not long ago, cash-flow forecasts were drawn up using pencil and paper – an extremely tedious job involving much rubbing out and re-entering of values. What-if analysis just was not feasible; it would have taken far too long. Now though, multiple versions of the same analysis can be produced in minutes. Just by changing a figure here or there, the formulae in the spreadsheet will re-calculate the whole analysis on the basis of the new figures, and the effect on the current account on the bottom line is displayed immediately.

Accessing, editing and saving

When you have developed your spreadsheet you will want to save it on disk. Otherwise it will be lost when you switch off or switch applications back to word processing for instance, or even clear the screen to work on another spreadsheet application. Remember, when you are interacting with data on the screen, that data only exists in the live memory circuits – the RAM of the computer.

Even if you don't anticipate needing the work again, you should save your work as a matter of course. It is so easy to do: with Lotus just type / to get the main menu, F for the file option, then S for save.

When you save a file you have to give it a name so you can call it back again if you need it. If you don't type in a file name when prompted to do so, the computer will do one of two things. It will either use the same file name you saved under before, or for a new file it will just call it FILE0001. However, it is much easier to find your work again if you give meaningful names to your files.

You have to be careful when saving an edited version of an old file, or you can lose the old version by overwriting it with the new version. If you want to keep the old and the new versions, be sure to give the new version a different name when prompted to do so during the Save command.

Recalling a file is easy. For instance with Lotus, once again choose the file option, and then within that, choose Retrieve. The keystrokes are /FR. This displays a list of the spreadsheet files available to choose from. Highlight the one you want and press <RETURN>. The computer recognizes spreadsheet files by an extension it attaches automatically when they are first saved. With later versions of Lotus the extension is .WK3. For instance if you choose to call your file CASHFLOW the file would actually appear on the disk directory as CASHFLOW.WK3

Graphs

The values produced by your spreadsheet can be displayed in a variety of ways as pie, bar, line and scatter diagrams for instance.

Each version of graphical output can also be named and saved separately, so it is possible to save several graphs as different ways of presenting information from the same spreadsheet. In the later versions of Lotus, these graphs are saved in the same file as, and are linked to, the spreadsheet itself. Thus if you change a value in the spreadsheet, a previously prepared graph will adjust in shape to accommodate the change.

Other software packages

There are many other types of software that you can buy to run on your PC which will allow you to use it for a great variety of different tasks. We cannot cover them all, so let us just take a quick look at six of the more common applications:

- Databases
- Accounting systems
- Project management software
- Computer-aided design (CAD)
- Desktop publishing
- Communications

Databases

The easiest way of understanding a database is to think of it performing rather like a kind of electronic card index system. Indeed there is a database package called Cardbox, but probably the better known ones are such products as dBase, Oracle and Dataease.

A computer database is far superior to the cardbox though. Not only does it automate the search procedure and do it in a tiny fraction of the time it would take to do manually, but it can also perform searches which would be almost impossible to do manually.

Here's a case in point. Long before computers were around, small businesses such as a local garage used to keep records in a card index. There would be a card for each customer, showing the customer's full name and address. The card might also hold other information such as the registration number of the cars owned by each customer, and perhaps a record of work done and invoices paid. The cards would be filed in alphabetical order of surname, so that a customer's records could be accessed quickly should the customer phone or call in.

But supposing a new mechanic needs to find out which customer owns a particular car on the forecourt with the registration number K 123 ABC for instance. The card index is very little help, because although all the registration numbers are held on the cards, the cards are in alphabetical order of surname, and that is what the mechanic is trying to find out! He could start searching through the index from the beginning, 'A's first, then 'B's and so on until he found it. But who will pay him for the hours it might take?

With a computer database however, you could key in either the customer's surname or the car registration number. The customer's record would appear just as quickly either way. This is the strength of the database. It holds information in such a way that you can search through it in all sorts of imaginative ways which would not be feasible with a card index system.

For instance suppose a sales representative keeps records of clients in his area. The records might show the name and address of the contact, the products bought, the date of the last visit and the value of orders placed during the last year. The sales representative might have an appointment in Hatfield and to make best use of his journey, could plan other visits in the same area. With a database it would be possible to list all customers in Hertfordshire. Or, if there were too many, the computer could be asked to display all customers in Hertfordshire who had not been visited in the last three months. Or perhaps better still, all customers in Hertfordshire, who had placed orders of greater than £10,000 in the last year, who had not bought product X and had not been visited in the last month.

These then are the type of queries that a database is designed to handle. As you can imagine, a card index would be next to useless for these kinds of search.

Accounting systems

Nearly every business, large or small, has one of these nowadays. Big organizations have big systems on the mainframe run by the finance department, while small businesses run a package such as Sage or Pegasus on their PC.

These packages make it possible to maintain up-to-date records of purchases, sales, stock levels, payrolls and timekeeping. The system will require purchase orders, invoices and wage slips to be produced using the system, and in this way the ledgers are all kept up to date automatically by the computer.

Apart from solving many of the filing problems associated with running a business, these packages also save much time in producing quarterly VAT tax returns, and the usual end of year Profit and Loss accounts, and Balance Sheets.

Most systems will also produce management reports, such as lists of stock items which are getting low, and lists of overdue debtors.

Project management software

If you are ever put in charge of a 'project' and you can work with a PC, get some project management software. It will pay for itself many times over.

So what is a project? Here are a few examples:

- Launching a new product or service.
- Overhauling operational equipment.
- Constructing a new building.
- Relocating an office.
- Installing a computer system.
- Conducting a training programme.

Thus any new work is a project if it lasts for a limited period, involves different groups and has penalties for late completion. The project manager is responsible for first planning, then controlling the allocation of time, money, people and other resources.

Managing a project is difficult because with new work there are few clear precedents to follow. Also, the people working on the project are often seconded part time and thus have other responsibilities and other bosses to please. So all in all, as a project manager you will need all the help you can get.

There are dozens of packages available. Some of the better known ones are Project Manager Workbench from Hoskyns, SuperProject Expert from Computer Associates, MacProject for the Apple Macintosh, and Artemis from Metier. They all require the project to be defined in terms of a list of the component activities which must be carried out, together with activity durations and dependency links.

The software then constructs a critical path network (see Chapter 2) and uses it as the basis for providing decision support for the project manager.

For instance, you can have a print-out of the activities shown as bars arranged on a Gantt chart, with the critical activities clearly indicated. Also, you can enter details of the resources allocated to each activity – the number of hours of each named person's time for instance – and get back a report of exactly when each resource is required.

Most packages can handle several projects all at the same time, and avoid conflicting demands being made for the same resource. Where conflicts do arise, the software makes it possible for you to re-run the analysis several times according to different priorities. Then after doing this what-if analysis, you can choose the most satisfactory alternative. This is really useful support – information processing at its most meaningful from a management point of view.

Computer aided design

Want to plan a new office layout? Or sketch an idea for a design? Then you will need a drawing board, a ruler for measuring, compasses, pencils and erasers . . . Or you could use a CAD package to develop your design on the screen of your PC before printing it.

CAD packages use just the same processes as your word processor or spreadsheet. Your work will be saved in files, and if you want to produce a design which is similar to something you have done before, you can save time by editing an old file.

Also you can mark a section of a drawing to repeat it or move it or delete it in much the same way as your word processor allows you to electronically cut and paste blocks of text. The only difference is that CAD packages are designed for manipulating graphics entities – arcs, lines, circles etc. – rather than text or numbers.

CAD packages can be awkward to use if the only input device you have is a keyboard. The keyboard was designed for inputting text and numerals, not graphics entities. For these you really need a mouse – a hand-held device you can move around on top of your desk. Then selecting a graphics entity is easy: you just point and click. Move the mouse and the cursor moves with it. You select from a pallette of graphics options displayed on the screen by pointing with the cursor and clicking the button on the mouse. Alternatively the mouse itself may be fitted with cross-hair sights which you aim over the desired pallette option mounted on a special tablet.

If you are thinking of buying a graphics package, you should know that there are a number of different types available, some of which make freehand sketching easy, and some which are more suitable for producing line drawings to scale for engineers and architects. Autocad is a well-known package for engineers and architects; Harvard Graphics is very popular in business for reports and presentations; and software with the words 'draw' or 'paint' in the title are usually more suitable for freehand work.

Desktop publishing

This is the software for you if you want to combine text and pictures to produce a newsletter or house magazine, or high quality reports and sales literature. In the past the only way was to write the text yourself and then get a typesetter and printer to design the page layout for you and print in the quantities you require. Now, with the right software and a suitable laser printer you can do it all yourself. However page layout is an art and you need an eye for design to produce really professional results.

Not long ago there was a big difference between word processors and desktop publishers. Now the gap has narrowed. Most modern word processors have some graphics capabilities and can set text in multiple columns in different fonts and typeface styles. Desktop publishing though can still offer much better ability to handle line and half-tone pictures. To get the half-tones into digital form you may need a scanner. Once you have the pictures on disk you can manipulate them just the same as other features to appear on the page: you can enlarge, contract, rotate, reproduce, relocate and so on.

Communications software

Most computers come with some form of primitive communications software built in to the operating system. This is to allow you to transfer files from one computer to another, or to allow your computer to act as a terminal connected to another, usually larger computer. However, you need to be something of a computer buff to make it all work. Setting up communications links between computers is best left to the experts: there are so many different protocols, or standards which must all match for the communication to work. So once you have got a link operating successfully, make sure you record the settings.

There is much more to communications than file transfer however. With suitable software and a modem, which we covered earlier when talking about networks, you can reach out through the telephone network to access data stored in remote databases. Doctors, engineers and scientists can scan research abstracts – and download (transfer to their own computer) the full text where appropriate. Business managers can scan the international news on particular subjects and capture stories they are interested in. Anyone can view real-time stock and share prices – and buy and sell through the network.

There's lots more too. You can send fax and telex messages, scan airline schedules and buy tickets, hire cars, and make hotel reservations worldwide.

One way is to subscribe to an information network such as Compuserve, an American company which claims to be the World's largest personal information service. For a modest fee they will supply the necessary software and provide a telephone helpline to get you started.

File organization

In this chapter we have mentioned files many times. As you know, all software and data and any work saved on disk is held in files. It is worth saying a few words about how these should be arranged so that you can find them again easily when necessary.

File names

At present the DOS operating system under which most PCs operate, requires that file names are restricted to a maximum of eight alphanumeric characters, plus an optional three character extension. For instance the following are all valid file names:

FILENAME.EXT
FILE.004
F.4
F2
F.2A8

You should not use spaces or full-stops in a filename, except for the full-stop just before the extension. Also for data files, you should not use filename extensions that the computer reserves for program files. The ones to avoid are: .COM .EXE .BAT .SYS.

For example the following file names would be invalid or likely to give trouble:

DAN.DARE
DARE DAN
CRICKET.BAT
KEEP OUT

There are a couple of other points worth bearing in mind about extensions.

First you should know that some packages automatically attach an extension to the file name you give to your data file. For instance, Lotus 1-2-3 attaches .WK3 (or for earlier versions .WK1) to the end of each file you save. Also, many word processors keep two copies of your files: one from the last time you saved your work, and the one from the time before last. This earlier copy is given the same filename as the file you are working on but is given the extension .BAK to indicate that it is a back-up copy in case you lose the latest version.

And the other point is that there are some loosely followed conventions applied by some programmers. They tend to use the extension to describe the type of file:

● README.TXT indicates that the file README is a text file that can be read directly through the operating system simply by typing at the prompt TYPE README.TXT This will cause the text in the file to be typed to the screen.
● CASHFLOW.BAS indicates that the file is a program written in the BASIC programming language.
● TEST.DAT indicates that the file contains data.

However these are not hard and fast rules, and you can make similar use of the extension if you choose. For instance you could use:

● JSMITH.LET for a letter to J Smith, and
● REPORT.423 for a report written on 23rd April.

Alternatively you can reserve the first one or two characters of the filename to code the files according to type:

● LJSMITH.001 for the first letter to J Smith, and MDJONES.004 for the fourth memo to D Jones, and RFBLOGGS.714 for the report to F Bloggs on 14th July.

The problem with coding is that the code letters reduce the available spaces in the file name, making it more difficult to build in meaning to the file name. The best way of overcoming this is to avoid relying entirely on a coding system, and physically store files of different types on different diskettes when you come to back up your files – that is prepare separate copies for archiving. You should then label and date the diskette, and store it in a box designed for the purpose. Then when you want to find a letter written to Mr Brown in October last year, you should know on which diskette to look for it.

The DIR command

The DOS operating system has a command DIR which allows you to list the names of files held on a disk. If you are logged on to disk drive

A: and you type DIR at the prompt, all files on the disk in drive A: will be listed. If you type DIR B: all the files on drive B will be listed.

That is useful, but if your diskette is nearly full it can produce a very long list of file names which you then have to scan through by eye. However there is a smarter approach which uses the 'wildcard' feature of DOS to narrow down the search to a much shorter list for you to scan by eye.

The wildcard characters are ? and *, which are used as follows:

● ? can be used to represent any single alphanumeric character, and * can be used to represent any group of alphanumeric characters.

They can be used in conjunction with DIR like this:

● Type DIR *.WK3 and the screen will display a list of all files with the .WK3 extension, which are Lotus files of course. Or, type DIR L*.714 and all files which start with an L followed by up to seven other characters and having an extension .714. Thus, if you are using L to indicate a letter file, and 714 to indicate 14 July, this command will call up all letters typed on that day. Or if you don't know the exact day in July, just type DIR L*.7* or DIR L*.7??

The extent you use this facility is limited only by the type of coding you adopt, and your imagination. One last example. Suppose you are looking for a letter, memo or report to Mr J. Smith, and the code you used was an L as the first character to indicate letter, M for memo and R for report. Then you could type DIR ?JSMITH??.* and the result will be a listing of all files with any character in the first place, and JSMITH in the next six places, and having any extension.

Disk directories

You may have a hundred or more files on a single floppy diskette, but it is common to have thousands of files on a hard disk. It is usual to divide up the hard disk into a kind of hierarchical structure of 'directories', within which files of different types can be saved.

When you switch to drive C: the hard disk, you will be in what is called the root directory, which is the one at the top of the hierarchy. It is normal to have separate directories at the first level down from the root, for word processing and spreadsheet applications, and any other software. Also, within and below say the word processing directory there will be another directory, two levels down from the root, to hold all the word processor work files to keep them separate from the software program files.

If you want to know more about directories, the best place to look is the DOS manual for your computer.

Competence self-assessment

1   What is the main application that managers use PCs for? Why is this inappropriate?

---

2   What proportion of managers use computers and networks to share information with their colleagues? But at the same time, what proportion of managers expect teleworking to form part of the future pattern of work?

---

3   If there are PCs where you work, find out the following about them:

- Are they networked?
- What software do they run? What is the name of the word processor, the spreadsheet, the database, and any other software?
- How much memory do the PCs have. That is, what size RAM in kilobytes or megabytes?
- What are they mostly used for?

---

4   Sit down at the keyboard of a PC, and see if you can carry out the following routine word processing functions. You will have to refer to the user guide to find the right commands for the particular word processor you are using. If possible, have someone around who can help if you get into difficulty.

(a) Switch on and start up the word processor.

(b) Type a few lines of text and save it under the filename MYFILE

(c) Copy your file to another file which you should call MYCOPY. You will have two versions of the same file on your disk now, identical in all respects except one is called MYCOPY and the other is called MYFILE

(d) Retrieve the file MYCOPY from disk. When you do this, the original stays on the disk and a duplicate is created in RAM which you can work on – edit and modify.

(e) Move the cursor through the text of your file. Find out how to move around quickly and precisely inside your document. Find out the commands for making the following moves:

- One character at a time, left and right.
- One word at a time, left and right.
- Jump to the margin, right and left.
- One line at a time, up and down.
- Jump to the top and bottom of the page.
- Jump to the beginning and end of the document.
- Find and jump forward to the next occurrence of a typed word or string of characters.

(f) Edit your file. Choose a word in the middle of your original text and delete it. Now add another word in its place. Add a new line or two of text at the end of the file.

(g) Save your edited file. You will find that the old version of MYCOPY on the disk will be replaced by the new, edited version.

---

5   Sit down at a PC equipped with spreadsheet software. Again you should have an experienced user around to help if at all possible.

(a) Switch on and start up the spreadsheet.

(b) In cell A1 type in a value, say 150. In cell A2 type in another value, say 25. In cell A3 type in (A1+A2) You should see the value 175 appear.

(c) In cell A4 type in your name.

(d) Use a simple spreadsheet command. For instance, call up the command menu. With Lotus this is done by pressing the / key. Now select the Copy command and copy the contents of cell A1 to cell D5.

(e) Now save your spreadsheet file. Clear your screen and check you can retrieve your saved file again.

(f) Quit and switch off.

References and further reading

British Institute of Management. *Management News* – (The newspaper of the British Institute of Management). BIM.

Lucey, T. (1991). *Management Information Systems* (6th edn). DP Publications.

Richards, I. (1989). *How to Use a Computer to Improve your Business*, Graham & Trotman.

Ross, P. W., Haiduk, H. P., Means, H. W. and Sloger, R. R. *Understanding Computer Information Systems*. West Publishing.

Sanders, D. H. (1988). *Computers Today* (3rd edn). McGraw-Hill.

5 Moulding the system to your needs

Why is this chapter relevant?

British managers are not famous for their long-term business planning and decision-making. The press often comments that our poor economic performance in the UK is in part due to short-termism. This may be true, but it is not clear what you or I should do about it: often we are forced into that mode by short-term financial targets imposed upon us.

However when it comes to management information systems (MIS) we really must plan ahead. To provide satisfactory customer service increasingly depends on making appropriate use of up-to-date technology, and the technology is developing at break-neck speed. It is verging on suicidal not to look ahead.

It is easy to overlook the staggering rate at which computers are developing – and costs continue to tumble. In the 1950s a Univac computer cost $2.5 million. By 1980 you could buy the same performance on a single circuit board costing $500. By comparison a Rolls-Royce costing $28,000 in 1950 should now cost $5 and run for three million miles on a single gallon of fuel.

The useful life of your information system at work – that network of computers which forms the nervous system of your organization – will last only for a few years. During the next five years or so, you will almost certainly be involved in the development or replacement of your system. This chapter will help you acquire a broader perspective, sounder judgement and greater confidence when making your contribution to new systems development.

The life cycle of an information system

Information systems don't just grow as a natural outcome of conducting business: they must be designed and installed by teams of specialists who know about business and also about computers. There are three main stages in a computer project:

- First, analysing how the business is run.
- Then designing on paper a suitable computer system.
- Then, buying the hardware, installing and using it.

To these three stages, we can add two more: a preliminary feasibility study before committing to the expense of a full-blown analysis of the business; and a final maintenance stage to keep the system running satisfactorily after it is installed. The complete systems life cycle therefore consists of five stages:

1 Feasibility study
2 Business analysis
3 Systems design
4 Implementation
5 Maintenance

The project team

If you work in a big organization with a computing department, you may be big enough to put together a project team entirely from your own staff. Smaller organizations however must get help from outside, preferably from reputable independent consultants. It is nice to be able to choose, but both approaches have their advantages.

Putting together your own project team is normally cheaper. Also, you keep the specialist knowledge in your organization and this can be useful in the later maintenance phase after the consultants have left. However, if you bring in consultants, you can benefit from their breadth of experience of analysing, designing and implementing systems in many other organizations. Thus your project will benefit from, and add to their experience as they pry into every corner of your business during the analysis phase. Of course their professional reputation is at stake so their confidentiality should be beyond question. The benefits of employing reputable consultants are that they can provide structure and methodology to the project. Also they represent additional human resources which are valuable to cover the extra work outside the normal run of your business during the middle stages of the project.

Even if you do employ consultants, you cannot hand the whole job to them: your staff must be well represented on the project team. The team will be led by a project manager, and should consist of:

● System users
● Business analysts
● Systems designers
● Computer programmers and engineers

Users are at the top of the list. They must get a system at the end which they had a big say in designing, and they feel they 'own'. Sometimes a misguided steering committee will try to impose a system without consulting the users sufficiently. This approach is very likely to fail; the best system in the world will fail if the users feel it is being used to spy on them or control them. They will use their ingenuity to find ways of defeating the system or circumventing it.

Another danger is that the computer professionals can get the bit between their teeth and charge off towards some technologically sophisticated dream solution. This too is likely to result in unsatisfactory performance. The users must believe in the benefits of the system and see it as a useful tool to help them do a better job.

It is the performance of the total human-computer system that matters, not just the computers. For the best chance of success the project team must gain total commitment and wholehearted co-operation from the users. Then the users will apply their ingenuity to make the system work, even if it turns out to be less than satisfactory from a purely technological point of view.

There is only one way of gaining the full support of users: they must be involved from the earliest stages of the project, all the way through to the end.

Organizing the project

The project manager will report directly to a steering committee consisting of senior executives (Figure 5.1). The direct costs of a major systems project will always be large, often a significant percentage of annual turnover. Also, the system may be essential for basic functions like invoicing and budgeting – activities to do with cash flow, the life-blood of the organization. There are very real risks if the system does not function satisfactorily, and so the steering committee must have the power of veto, to halt the project at the end of any one of the five stages of the project. The project team must therefore prepare a report for the steering committee at the end of each stage, with two or three

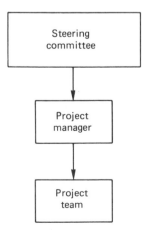

Figure 5.1 *Project organization chart*

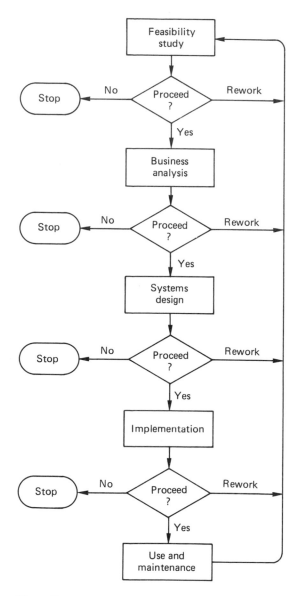

Figure 5.2 *Steering committee control of project*

suggestions for the next stage, one of which should be recommended for approval by the steering committee (Figure 5.2).

We will return to examine how the project is controlled through the five stages of the life cycle, but first, let us review how computers initially came to be used in business. Technology is still developing very rapidly and has a big influence on the design of information systems, so to get a feel for where business computing is headed, you should know where it came from.

The birth and upbringing of the business computer

Conception

In 1958 there were just 160 computers in the whole of Europe, and only the very biggest companies could even think about using them – mostly for scientific applications. All organizations used paperwork systems for recording and distributing the information they needed. These systems were operated by an army of clerks, secretaries, mail boys and teams in finance with the strange title of 'comptometer operator', who spent the day tapping away on adding machines. Information was stored in filing cabinets and plan chests, accessed by asking a secretary to pull out the needed files or drawings, and communicated through circulation lists and the internal mail system.

Embryo

By the late 1950s some businesses were waking up to the potential of these computers operated by scientists. Computers at that time were huge, unreliable monsters consuming so much power that the lights dimmed when they were switched on. They relied on thousands of radio valves that popped and fused like light bulbs. The machines seldom ran for more than a few hours between failures, and needed special premises and a large team of engineers to keep them going.

However some businesses discovered that they could save on labour costs by buying time on these machines. They got access at economic rates to the number-crunching power of the scientists' computers, which proved ideal for routine accounting functions. The first business uses they were put to were the processing of payrolls and accounts receivable. Big savings were made in labour by automating clerical tasks and one of the first jobs to disappear was that of the comptometer operator.

Birth

During the 1960s organizations began to realize that computers could be applied to other routine tasks such as stock control and production control. Transistors replaced radio valves, making computers cheaper and more reliable, and so bigger companies began to set up their own data processing departments and operate their own computers. Thus the central mainframe was borne, operated by DP staff offering a computing service to other department managers.

Infancy

By the late 1970s more and more business tasks were being computerized. The transistor which had replaced the radio valve was itself being replaced, first by the integrated circuit and then by the microprocessor. These developments cut the costs of computing dramatically while at the same time increasing their power and reliablility.

Also, many department managers were beginning to get fed up with going cap in hand to the DP citadel to beg small computing favours. They were beginning to find that computers were simple enough to run and had fallen in price sufficiently for them to buy and operate in their own departments, which freed them from being dependent on the DP department. Separate computers were soon arriving in the Design Offices, the Planning Department, the Sales Office and so on.

This piecemeal approach to corporate computing came about because managers could make immediate savings in direct labour at the same time as freeing themselves from dependence on the DP department. Naturally the DP departments did what they could to resist this trend, because they could see their influence waning. But it was too late. The arrival of the PC in the early 1980s reduced even further the significance of the big central mainframe. The low cost and versatility of the PC meant they were popping up like mushrooms, everywhere.

Soon computers were to be found in nearly every organization.

However, this could hardly be called a corporate approach to computing. The PCs were being used to automate the old paperwork systems, faults and all, and were reinforcing departmental boundaries. Each computer held its own separate files. The same information was being held many times over in different computers, with some versions obviously being more up to date than others. And to transfer data from one department to another involved printing out hard copy in the sending department and then re-keying the printed data back into the computer at the receiving department.

Adolescence

Today these so-called 'islands of automation' – separate computers in different departments – are being linked together via communications networks to form management information systems. The intention is that these integrated systems of computers should transcend departmental boundaries and allow data to be held at different points in the network, and yet be available through the network to all authorized users who might need it.

There is a concept known as single data entry for multiple users. In theory it means that each data element held by the total system should only be held once. In practice it is interpreted to mean that there should be the least possible duplication in the storage of data. If data is only entered and held once, in a single common database, there can only be one version of the state of play, available to all who need it. This will eliminate the confusions that can arise when earlier versions of modified records or drawings are allowed to remain in circulation.

In fact if a 'bottom up' implementation by many managers acting independently has progressed too far, it may pre-empt any 'top down' planning for a corporate approach to the information needs of the organization as a whole. The many different hardware types, operating systems, and incompatible software bought by different managers will make it almost impossible to link them up.

Business computing has yet to mature. It is still going through a dynamic period of growth and development. It can only be said to have matured when a set of standards have been developed for all manufacturers and users (like for cars, for instance), and development has slowed down. This is unlikely to happen for some years yet.

Controlling a computer system project

Let us start with an overview of the size of team required and the costs involved at different stages of the project (Figure 5.3).

Phase	Team size	Typical proportion of total project costs (%)
Feasibility study	1 or 2 analysts	<5
Business analysis	Project manager + 3 or 4 analysts	10–15
System design	Project manager + analysts + programmers + users	25–30
Implementation	Project manager + analysts + programmers + users	55–60

Figure 5.3 *Team size and costs for each project phase*

The feasibility study

This is a first quick look at the suitability of current methods of handling information, to see if they need modifying or changing. It involves only a few business analysts and systems designers.

The level of expenditure is very low, consisting of little more than the cost of the time logged by these individuals. Clearly no programming skills are needed at this stage – in fact the project manager and team will not yet be recruited. Even so, it is important that the potential users of the new system are kept fully informed of the purpose of the study, and the opportunities for participation if the project goes ahead.

The feasibility study stage should close with a report to senior management, with a recommendation and alternative proposals, complete with an investment analysis consisting of an estimated internal rate of return and payback period.

A recommendation by senior management for the project to proceed will commit the organization to the costs of setting up the steering committee, appointing a project manager, and seconding members onto the project team. There will also be consultants' fees and other indirect costs.

The feasibility study should also provide senior management with a rough estimate of total project costs, which in principle they should be prepared to sanction if they recommend the project to proceed.

The business analysis

This will not involve any capital costs. The project is still at the investigation stage and can be thought of as a re-run in more detail of the feasibility study.

In fact this stage of the project will be concerned with three basic issues:

- Business objectives and philosophy.
- What is done now, and how it is done.
- What should be done, and how it could be done.

The type of skill required to investigate these issues is slightly different in each case. An experienced manager with business skills is required for the first phase, especially if there has been no corporate planning or formal statement of corporate objectives, as is often the case with young companies.

Does the organization set out to provide a high specification product at a high price? – or a mid-range service competing on price? And how are these objectives to be achieved? By keeping tight control of bad debts? By monitoring closely the relationship between price and sales volume? Answers are needed to questions such as these, to use as system design criteria.

A systems analyst is needed to determine what is done now by the organization, and what procedures it uses. The systems analyst will analyse the organization as a system and study its inputs, the processes it performs on the inputs, and the outputs. Some of the inputs will be information in one form or another, while other inputs will be more tangible, such as raw materials or products.

The systems analyst will collect a complete set of all manual pro-forma paperwork used for purchasing, invoicing, production and any other purposes. These are important indicators to how the organization functions. Procedures manuals and information system documentation are also useful guides to what was intended should be done. Interviews with staff will establish just how well the procedures manuals correspond with what is actually done in practice, and the reasons for the departure from standard practice.

The kinds of skill required here are interviewing skills and an understanding of business procedures, paperwork systems and computer systems.

The last phase of the business analysis, that of establishing what should be done and how, relates to the two previous phases. Procedures should relate directly to the corporate objectives and philosophy. However, in the interest of keeping change to a minimum, the best of the present system should be preserved whereever possible.

This phase requires some technical knowledge as well as business analysis skills. It may be necessary to start making initial contacts with manufacturers and suppliers of systems at this stage.

It will be necessary to second more team members in order to bring together for this stage a sufficiently broad spectrum of skills and knowledge in the project team. As a rough guide, it would not be unusual for the business analysis stage of the project to consume a fifth of the total team man-hours over the life of the project.

We have called this stage business analysis: in fact it is often referred to as systems analysis because the business is analysed as a system, and then the systems the business uses – and could use – are analysed. It requires some knowledge of technology that is available and lays the groundwork for the next stage of the project, the systems design.

Systems design

All the investigation work has now been completed and the results of these should be available as the 'deliverables' from the business analysis stage, in the form of reports and documentation. These then form the basis for drawing up a full technical specification. If possible it should not be hardware specific, so that different manufacturers and suppliers can be invited to tender against the specification.

When the steering committee gives the go-ahead for this stage, the project will gain further momentum, using perhaps a third of the total team hours during the life of the project. The team will grow as some initial input from programmers and engineers will be required. As well as hardware, software will be needed, which may consist of proven off-the-shelf packages, but for larger applications it is probable that at least some of the software will have to be written specially. The software will not be bought in or written until the next stage, that of implementation, but to prepare the way systems software specifications must be drawn up.

Implementation

This is the major part of the project and it is when the largest expenditure occurs. Half the total project team hours may be used at this stage, and there will be large capital costs for hardware and software. Also, there will be training costs which typically may be similar in size to the hardware costs.

This is also the stage at which the major risks occur. Up to this point, there has been no interference with the basic procedures that the organization uses to conduct its affairs. But now it is planned to transfer operations to the new system. Inevitably there will be a 'J-curve' effect where output dips during and immediately after the transfer. This must be expected, but if all goes well, output should quickly recover to a new higher level, and this too must be anticipated by making sure inputs are adequate to sustain the new higher level of output (Figure 5.4).

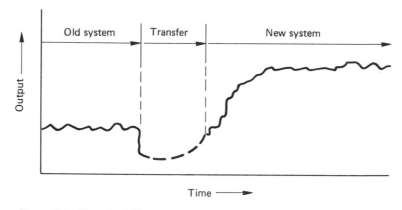

Figure 5.4   *The output 'J'-curve*

The big risk of course is that all may not go well, and the steering committee must be very confident that the system will work. They may require the project team to confirm that all is well before authorizing transfer of operations to the new system.

The main phases of implementation are:

- Hardware purchase and installation.
- Software purchase and writing.
- Systems and software testing.
- User training.
- File conversion and transfer to the new system.
- Switch to the new system and stop using the old system.

Hardware purchase and installation

This will involve inviting suppliers to tender against the technical specification, but inevitably suppliers will emphasize their strengths, and not dwell on the shortcomings of their tender. The project team must make sure that no important areas of weakness are overlooked.

Installation is bound to cause some disruption as ceiling panels are taken down and floors lifted to install communications cabling.

Software purchase and writing

Comparing and assessing the suitability of different packages is quite a complex business. Technical conformance to the specification is obviously important, but the user-friendliness of the human-computer interface is extremely important. The computer experts, because of their familiarity with the way computers work, are sometimes not aware of the difficulties new users have with new systems. These difficulties can be overcome by training, but an inherently difficult system will from the start cause irritation and will never endear itself to the users.

Even standard off-the-shelf software must be installed on the hardware and set up to produce the type of output required. However users are not always able to describe exactly the type of support they require from the system, until they start using it. Then they can recognize it when they see it.

In these circumstances, prototyping is appropriate. The programmer uses a fourth generation programming language, a 4GL, to produce very quickly a limited package with keyboard inputs and screen outputs which can easily be changed. Then when the user is satisfied, the programmer can go away and write the full version. This will take longer to do than the prototype version, but will have adequate speed and capacity to meet the design specification.

Systems and software testing

When the hardware and software for all the component sub-systems have been installed and tested, the whole system including all computerized and manual procedures must be tested to ensure it operates in an integrated fashion.

In a big systems project testing can never guarantee perfection because of the almost infinite number of multiple interrelationships that can arise between program modules. However, common human and physical failures can be anticipated and so these are purposely introduced. During a test run, erroneous transactions are processed and hardware failures are simulated to check that the system can handle the problem and recover from the failure.

User training

Skimping on training is a false economy, and yet, if the project budget is under pressure, training is more likely to be cut than hardware. The technology cannot work without people: people form the most important part of the total system.

The trouble lies deep in management attitudes which are reinforced by our financial accounting conventions. Hardware appears as assets on the balance sheet, whereas people don't, so despite claims from the top that 'people are our most important asset', training is not seen as an investment. The government does not help either; they award much more money in grants for equipment than they do for training.

Also, hardware cannot walk away, whereas people can. A typical British manager's attitude is that if you give people training, they are sure to leave because they can use it to secure a better job. This is in stark contrast to the experience of Nissan who have big budgets for on-going training. They know that people will actually decide to stay with them because there are opportunities for training, rather than move and get stuck in a job where there is no training. When Nissan opened a plant in Tennessee, USA, they spent $30,000 per employee on training before the plant started operation.

If money spent on training is not money down the drain, then what is the pay-off? There's the rub: the benefits are very difficult to estimate, even with specific operator training. The costs of training are up-front and known exactly, but how can you ever know whether it was worthwhile? All you can do is rely on the advice of consultants with experience of systems projects where greater and lesser amounts were spent on training. They should be able to estimate the savings that arise from shorter start-up and improved system effectiveness.

The documentation produced during the analysis and design stages of the project will provide a rich source of training material.

File conversion and transfer

The files of standing data used by the old system must be copied over to the new system before the new system can operate. For instance, the file of customer addresses, and the file of product prices are needed before the system can produce invoices. It is seldom as simple as loading a tape from the old system and getting the new system to read it. Usually there will be hardware or software incompatibilities which make that impossible. Special programs will have to be written to translate the old tapes into a form understandable by the new system.

If a manual procedure used before as part of the previous system is to be computerized, then any necessary manual data will need to be keyed in manually.

The transfer of files must not take too long however, because life goes on during the transfer and the old system will continue to be used for business until the final switch-over. Thus the state of play on the old system will advance, and the taped data put into the new system will soon be out of date. This will make switching over to the new system difficult because it is not up to date.

Switching to the new system and stopping the old system.

Wherever possible a phased implementation should be adopted, with different sub-systems brought on-line one at a time. With modern real-time systems which rely on a single database, it is not possible to reduce the risks in this way: the whole system must be started at the same time.

Another way to reduce the risks is to use a period of parallel operation as a safeguard to check that the new system is functioning correctly, before switching off the old system. This should be for a strictly limited period, because maintaining both systems doubles the work load for the users with every transaction having to be input twice. Also, it prevents the users from gaining confidence in the new system. With both systems running, users will revert to the old system whenever there is a difficulty.

The project team should encourage ownership of the system by the users, and should reduce support to normal maintenance levels soon after the old system is abandoned.

Maintenance

This is included as one of the stages in the life cycle of the system, but it is not part of the project, because it will last for years, up to the time when a new feasibility study marks the beginning of the next systems project.

The purpose of system maintenance is not to maintain the status quo, like car maintenance for instance. Maintenance in the context of information systems means maintaining a system which is appropriate to the business needs of the organization. There will be occasions when a system 'bug' requires fixing, but for the most part, maintenance is more a question of adjusting the system to suit the changing needs of the organization over time.

A change in the rate for value added tax is one example of the kind of influence that may result in a need for system maintenance. The program that computes the amount of VAT charged on invoices will need to be edited.

One of the project team's last responsibilities is to conduct a post-implementation review. The purpose of this is to compare the performance of the system with what was originally specified in the systems design documentation. As a result, before finally being disbanded, the team may be asked by users to do some post-implementation fine-tuning of the system.

Apart from acting as an important control activity, the post-implementation review is a valuable opportunity for team members to learn from the experience of being involved with the project. It will add to their value as team members on the next project.

ORACLE at work

Testing the ORACLE

Test Valley Borough Council's housing department is reaching the end of an extensive software development which will provide the department with a comprehensive system for maintenance and rent collection on council properties.

John Spens, principal assistant chief housing officer, at Test Valley, appointed a small working party at the end of 1989 to investigate the software packages currently on the market but, after four months, concluded that there was nothing suitable for his housing department. 'Our primary criterion was excellence, but, like all local councils, we needed to find a cost-effective solution.'

'We visited several other councils to discuss the solutions that they had implemented, but this failed to turn up anything suitable for our purposes.' Currently all thirteen authorities in Hampshire have different systems in place.

Test Valley is replacing two separate systems with a single integrated solution; a 15-year-old rent system which was originally jointly developed for Test Valley and Winchester City Council, and DILIS, a maintenance system purchased from ICL in 1984. The council properties to be included are all houses, flats, and garages in the council's ownership as well as properties which are on short term leases.

Spens' next step was to arrange for an initial specification of the system to be prepared. This was then sent to five different software houses including ORACLE and PIC. 'As a housing department we had little previous experience of Oracle and invited them to tender on the strength of the company's reputation and recommendations received from other users,' said Spens.

'PIC and Oracle decided to offer a joint bid which was excellent news for us, as it meant combining PIC's extensive expertise in housing with Oracle's strength in IT as a leading software company,' said Spens.

The Oracle/PIC bid was accepted by Test Valley Borough Council in September 1990 and the companies started work on developing a complete turnkey system for the department.

Using Oracle's CASE methodology the development team started with three months of analysis in defining the scope of the system. 'Although we had supplied quite a detailed specification there was a lot of fine detail to be decided,' explained Spens.

Around ten users at Test Valley were involved in this analysis stage. In addition to Spens and the project manager the other users came from various sections of the Housing Department, such as Rent Arrears, Rent Accounting, Estate Management, Responsive Maintenance and Programmed Maintenance.

'Initially, the users were rather sceptical about the system, but they were soon won over as they found how much power to influence the system lay in their hands,' explained Peter Bird, the project manager. 'Very often users are simply handed a system with little previous consultation and told to get on with it.'

'The CASE methodology was extremely useful in building confidence levels. Using the diagramming techniques all the users were able to understand the scope and direction the system was taking and a lot of valuable feedback was gleaned in the early stages.'

Context sensitive help

'We have put a high priority on making the system as intuitive and easy to use as possible. Additionally there is a large degree of context sensitive help available to users on line which has also allayed many of their fears,' Bird continued.

The timescales were set for May 1992 for the repairs element of the system to go live and December 1992 for the rents. At present everything is on line for these targets and the project is currently in the build phase with an accompanying increase in activity level. There is a total of twenty-three people working on the project.

'There will be forty-two terminals in the department which will be connected to the system giving almost all staff desktop access,' said Bird.

Intensive training

Intensive training is planned during November 1992 for all users and the systems will be run in tandem for two weeks in order to ensure data integrity and that there are no hiccups in going live.

The system will include approximately 100 modules and can be divided into three areas, estate management, repairs and rent. The estate management segment keeps all details of properties, which includes statistical information on accommodation, number of bedrooms, garden sizes and many other attributes useful for repairs such as window frames, roof tiles, plumbing and central heating. Much of the information to fill this database will be transferred from the current system. Whenever repair orders are issued and completed, attributes are automatically changed so that information is always up-to-date.

The second segment deals with repairs and provides the complete system for inputting and managing 40,000 repair jobs every year. The system holds a schedule of rates for different jobs so that the best contractors can be selected for each repair task. Details of when jobs are issued, to whom and what priority rating they have been assigned are also included.

'We are expecting a big improvement in service to our customers as management information will be far better. The system will supply us with details on how reliable contractors are, how many jobs each has been issued with, whether targets are being met and where any hold-ups are occurring.'

The third and final part deals with rents and will handle the rental income of £14m per annum and will particularly assist with the recovery of rent arrears.

'Rent assistants will have access to complete and up-to-date records of rent payments and will be able to select one of twenty different standard letters held on file. These are automatically generated but can be tailored or personalized if appropriate. Additionally, we will be able to generate statements of account on demand with a few keystrokes. These will include all payments, details of housing benefit, credits and debits.'

The computer will play an important role in monitoring arrangements for reducing rent arrears and individual schedules for payment. The system will alert the department if there is a deviation from the agreed payment plan. Another useful feature is the system's calendar which keeps a note of when Notice of Seeking Possessions are issued and will alert the department when they are due to expire.

'Test Valley has a good record on rent arrears anyway,' admits Spens, 'but now it should be even better.'

A lot of attention was devoted to the design of the system so that it will interface perfectly with other systems which are renewed or replaced in the future.

Five year pay back

Spens estimates that the system will pay for itself within five years on a straight financial basis, without considering the improved service and efficiency. 'There were very high costs associated with running DILIS on the Council's mainframe. ICL DRS 6000 hardware with ORACLE is a far more cost-effective solution.'

'As well as the financial justification there are a number of other benefits, which we will gain,' explained Spens. 'Firstly, the system will be completely up-to-date with a very high degree of applicability, financial and management information. It will be far easier to access and reports can be generated either on an *ad hoc* basis or as standard, planning and budgetary control will be vastly improved and many of the tasks that could previously only be achieved after hours of manual work can be completed in a matter of minutes.'

As far as the system's life cycle is concerned Spens admits that it is virtually impossible to predict this but he confidently expects the ORACLE system to withstand the next fifteen years at least: 'Rent accounting has hardly changed over the past decade. However, one can't predict legislative changes and "future-proofing" is important.'

'We are very optimistic about the improvements that the new integrated system will bring and feel confident about the decision we have made,' concluded Spens.

Competence self-assessment

1 List the five stages in the life cycle of a management information system project. Write a couple of lines describing the purpose of each stage. Sketch a graph to show how cost and effectiveness vary over the life of a system.

2 Describe the membership of the project team. What skills are required, and at which stages are the different skills required? When should system users be involved?

3 What are the advantages and disadvantages of employing external consultants on a systems project?

4 Describe the organizational structure, and procedures for the overall control of the project. When do the major risks and costs occur, and how are they monitored and controlled?

5 Describe the four main stages in the development of the use of computers for business purposes. What problems have arisen from this development, and how might they be overcome?

6   Why is single data entry for multiple users thought to be an important principle in the design of management information systems?

7   What are the three main areas of investigation in a business analysis conducted as part of a systems project? Briefly describe the sources that should be examined in these three areas.

8   List the six major tasks that make up the implementation stage of a systems project. Write a couple of lines to describe the purpose of each task.

References and further reading

Lucey, T. (1991). *Management Information Systems* (6th edn). D P Publications.
Richards, I. (1989). *How to use a computer to improve your business*. Graham & Trotman.
Ross, P. W., Haiduk, H. P., Means, H. W. and Sloger, R. R. *Understanding Computer Information Systems*. West Publishing.

6 Information around the world and into the future

Why is this chapter relevant?

This chapter looks beyond today and the immediate boundaries of your organization, to see where the current trends are leading.

Networks are enmeshing the whole world. They are changing the ways we do business, opening up new opportunities and presenting new threats. The changes are real, critical to success and survival, and sure to have a major impact on your work.

To prepare yourself and your organization for the world of tomorrow, you need to know what is happening. By reading this chapter you can increase your awareness of developments reported in the press, and perhaps be in a better position to understand their implications.

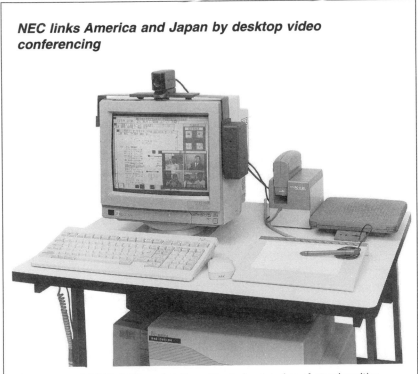

NEC links America and Japan by desktop video conferencing

Figure 6.1 *A MERMAID workstation with window interface, electronic writing pad, image scanner, video camera and telephone attached (courtesy NEC Corporation)*

NEC Corporation has developed an international teleconferencing system, based on a network of special workstations which incorporate a small television camera. Users on the network have access to a central database and can communicate with each other in real-time by voice and video pictures, while sharing a joint view of their work which may be in the form of text, graphics, scanned images and hand drawings.

NEC's system, called MERMAID, makes it possible for people on different continents to work as a group, interacting in real-time with their shared work (Figure 6.1). NEC is now using the system between their headquarters in Tokyo and four research centres – three in Japan and one in America. To make the system possible, NEC scientists had to develop a new multimedia communications protocol for use on ISDN networks, and computer networks, including Internet, the international computer network

MERMAID, which stands for multimedia environment for remote multi-attendee interactive decision-making, allows real international group work between any number of participants from anywhere in the world where there is a workstation linked to the network.

This must be one of the most advanced examples of groupware, or computer supported cooperative work (CSCW), and it can be used for:

● Cooperative software development.
● Group decision support.
● Interactive education and training.
● Financial trading support.
● Joint authoring and document editing.
● Home working.
● Remote information retrieval from multi-media databases.

NEC views this new network as the first step towards the creation of a global multimedia communications system which will link not only Japan and the United States, but all regions of the world creating a truly global communications network.

Information and the global marketplace

Kenichi Ohmae, the managing director in Japan of the international management consultants McKinsey, has written a book about how the world of commerce has become almost borderless. In his book, *The Borderless World*, Ohmae, who is one of the leading writers on corporate planning, is concerned that too few managers are developing truly global strategies.

'On a political map, the boundaries between countries are as clear as ever. But', says Ohmae, 'on a competitive map, a map showing the real flows of financial and industrial activity, those boundaries have largely disappeared. Of all the forces eating them away, perhaps the most persistent is the flow of information.'

We are becoming global citizens. Turn on your TV and you will see shots of people in the streets of Belgrade, Moscow, Baghdad, Tokyo, Hong Kong, Paris, New York . . . We can all see for ourselves people in the streets of cities all around the world. We see their choice of clothes, the cars they drive – their preferences in fashion, sports and lifestyles. And news reporters always seem to be able to find someone who speaks English, because it seems English is becoming the common language of the global citizen.

Within big corporations, this globalization is even more advanced. Executives dress the same, use similar offices and equipment, drive similar cars, operate similar machines – and mostly speak English. This makes it easy for executives to switch corporations and switch countries.

Ohmae believes that 'When information flows with freedom, the old geographic barriers become irrelevant. Global needs lead to global products. For managers, this flow of information puts a high premium on learning how to build the strategies and the organizations capable of meeting the requirements of a borderless world.' Myopic managers with limited, parochial ambitions will lose out in this new global marketplace.

So far we have been talking about information in the public domain – available to all of us through personal observation. But the volume of private information flowing unobserved between countries and ignoring national boundaries is also growing rapidly, roughly doubling every six years.

This private information flows through private international networks, set up for specific purposes. For instance, the world's major banks belong to a private network, the Society for Worldwide Interbank Financial Transactions (SWIFT), which allows subscribers to make a transaction half way round the world and have it acknowledged within a few seconds. The system handles transactions worth hundreds of billions of pounds on a typical day, and this is just one network amongst several others serving the banking sector, such as the Clearing House for International Payments (CHIPS) and the Clearing House Automated Payment System (CHAPS).

There are hundreds of other private networks to handle all manner of different information types. There are networks for electronic mail, airline seat reservations, meteorological data, international news services, and the export of information services – to name but a few.

Generally the networks are constructed around a mainframe database, with remote access available through the network, most of which consists of leased lines, satellite links and submarine cables operated by bulk carriers. The older networks are based around traditional telephone technology, but the newer networks are digital, offering much greater capacity, accuracy and speed.

In the UK, network operators offer their services through British Telecom or Mercury transmission lines. Both have two different types of line: the old telephone wire lines which are designed for speech, and the new Integrated Services Digital Network (ISDN) fibre optic cables which can carry not only digitally coded text and graphics but also voice and moving video.

Electronic data interchange (EDI)

EDI is a generic term to describe a network setup between a purchasing organization and its suppliers, to speed up the process of making enquiries, placing orders, invoicing and settling accounts. The original idea was to get rid of the paperwork by taking the digital purchasing information from the purchaser's computer, and inputting it directly into the supplier's computer. Potentially this would be faster and less prone to typographical errors.

British Coal – A case study

In 1990 British Coal sent out 600,000 purchase orders and received 1.6 million invoices. They stocked over 200,000 different product lines. They had been working with their suppliers, to set up EDI links and by 1990 had 500 of them on-line, enabling British Coal to place one third of their orders electronically.

This allowed the lead-time between placing an order and receiving the goods, to be reduced by two weeks. Stock levels could then be reduced by £1m, and reduced paper handling is estimated to have saved a further £50,000. Another benefit is that suppliers' costs are lower, and as a result, British Coal has been able to negotiate lower purchase prices.

Setting up direct communications between computers is always tricky and in the early days of EDI, there were no nationally defined standards. It was easiest to implement if both trading partners had the same hardware and software. The digital data could then be transferred by direct communications link, or by physical exchange of tapes or disks.

As the idea caught on, more organizations wanted to join in, and often they had incompatible systems. To make it possible, the parties had to agree a specific data format for the exchange, and one or both would then have to convert their data to that format before communicating.

Soon, third party network operators stepped in, to act as electronic clearing houses. Their networks are called value added networks or VANs, as opposed to LANs or WANs, because their networks incorporate a computer and database which allows each company to have its own electronic mailbox through which it can send and receive messages.

To send a message to one of its trading partners, a company must first convert the message into the format required by the VAN, using software provided by the VAN. The network is dialled up and the message sent off.

On receipt of the message, the VAN simply places it into the intended recipient's mailbox. The recipient then dials up the network to access the mailbox and downloads the messages into its own internal computer system. The recipient must also have software to convert the data back from the VAN format into its own format.

The three main EDI VAN operators in the UK are:

- INS who offer TRADANET and other services, who have about two thirds of the market.
- ISTEL, owned by AT & T, who offer EDICT, and have about a quarter of the market.
- IBM who offer Managed Network Services, with about 10 per cent of the market.

INS has more customers than the other two. In addition to TRADANET which is designed for the retail and distribution sectors, INS offers PHARMANET (pharmaceuticals), MOTORNET (automotive) and several others.

ISTEL, originally formed by British Leyland, still has most of its customers in the engineering and manufacturing sectors, but is expanding into health, finance, retail and distribution.

IBM has the smallest market share, but has been chosen by the National Health Service to be its network provider. The NHS is one of the world's biggest purchasers with thousands of suppliers who will eventually have to set up EDI links through IBM's Managed Network Services.

The UK is well ahead of Europe in using EDI. More than seventy of *The Times* Top 100 companies use EDI, and about two thirds of all European EDI activity is here in the UK. As users in world markets we are second only to the USA.

However, our lead has resulted in a plethora of incompatible systems. In addition to the three VAN operators in the UK there are several industrial groups who have agreed messaging standards for electronic trading. For instance:

- CEFIC in the chemical industry.
- EDIFICE in the electronics industry.
- ODETTE in the automotive industry.
- EDICON in the construction industry.

Worldwide however, there are three leading standards emerging:

- In the UK it is the TRADACOMS (Trading Data Communications) standard, as they have the biggest customer base of over 2000 users.
- In the USA it is ANSI ASC X.12 (American National Standards Institute).
- Internationally it is UN/EDIFACT (United Nations/Electronic Data Interchange for Administration, Commerce and Transport). It is new and in 1991 had only developed standards for one message, the purchase order, compared to TRADACOMS' sixteen, but has received wide endorsement from companies and governments around the world.

So what should new users do? In the UK it will probably be necessary to develop systems that can handle both the TRADACOMS and the EDIFACT standards.

The Data Protection Act 1984

What would you think if you were refused life insurance though perfectly fit? Or inexplicably refused credit? Or failed to get a job because the interviewer somehow knew of your past membership of a political party or trade union? Would you be disturbed if on responding by phone to an advertisement, you find the salesman knows who you are without being told? Would it upset you if he also knows your age, the credit cards you use, and the fact that you spend most weekends away in Brighton?

You would rightly be outraged and extremely alarmed if you found that details, perhaps erroneous, of your medical, financial and personal life were in general circulation and being used against you. But technically this Big Brother scenario is feasible right now, and the only protection you and I as individuals have is the Data Protection Act, which by curious coincidence was passed in 1984.

It has always been possible to use technology for good or evil, and this time it is database technology which we must channel in the right direction. Organizations use databases to keep records of their customers, clients, patients, members, shareholders, students etc. together with their addresses and details of transactions of various types. Every time you join a professional association, buy shares, fill in a guarantee card or book a holiday, your name and address and details of the transaction are added to a database. On their own these records pose no threat to you but if they are brought together, cross-referenced and compared, they reveal a detailed picture of your habits and lifestyle which should remain private.

Databases are stored on disk and in computer memory, and the cost per kilobyte of storage has roughly halved every two years since business computers were first used. This phenomenon shows every sign of continuing, and it is now ecomomic to store millions of records, any one of which can be accessed in seconds. An obvious application in this era of the credit card, is the running of instant creditworthiness checks. If you make a large purchase with your Access or Visa card, the salesperson will phone up the credit card company to check the status of your account. It takes seconds for the computer to access your account number from amongst the millions of others.

The world of business has not been slow to see the potential from a marketing point of view. By buying and selling lists of different types and bringing them together into a single database, selective searches can be made to produce lists of potential customers who conform to some desired profile. There is no point trying to sell to a person who hasn't the money or use for your product. For instance suppose you want to sell compact disks by direct mail. If you mail just to prospects who have recently bought a CD player (and filled in the guarantee card), and also have lots of disposable income (they buy shares), they are much more likely to buy.

Direct mail organizations can dramatically improve their response rates by mailing only to sub-sets of list entries which conform to certain defined requirements. There are companies which buy lists from all sorts of different sources and then sell their services to other companies for credit checking and marketing purposes.

For instance, one such company, CCN Systems in Nottingham, is an offshoot of Great Universal Stores. It holds millions of records – different lists from different sources, which can be cross-referenced, compared and related. Their computer holds a list of every address in the UK plus thirty million financial details and 2.5 million personal profiles. Their sources include government census information, council electoral roles, the Post Office postal address file and county court records of bad payers. This mix of socio-economic, demographic and geographic information works so well that CCN Systems is now a multi-million pound company, trading lists with other companies and selling their credit checking and marketing services.

CCN Systems operate to standards which go beyond those required by the Data Protection Act of 1984, but databases of personal details are built and swapped around between companies so frequently now, that it is getting difficult to keep track of where details came from originally. The individual is at a distinct disadvantage in any dealings with the big database users. The Data Protection Act was passed in 1984 to safeguard the interests of the individual and guard against the improper use of personal data.

The Act also allows the UK to ratify the Council of Europe Convention on Data Protection. The Convention was agreed to ensure that data can flow freely between all European countries. Our Act therefore plays a role in protecting our international trade.

There are eight internationally agreed principles of data protection which form the basis for the 1984 Act. Data must be registered with the Data Protection Registrar, and personal data must be:

1 Obtained fairly and lawfully.
2 Only held for lawful registered purposes.
3 Only used or disclosed for registered purposes.
4 Adequate, relevant and not excessive for registered purposes.
5 Accurate and up to date.
6 Not kept longer than necessary.
7 Made available to data subjects on request.
8 Properly protected against loss or disclosure.

The Act applies only to computer-held data and sets only a minimal framework of standards. Also, it is difficult to see how it can be effectively enforced. For instance, you are entitled as an individual data subject to see what information is held about you – if you know who to ask! But, unless it is inaccurate or otherwise in breach of the Act you are not entitled to have it changed or erased, or prevent it being passed on to other data users. Also, you are not entitled to know where the data came from in the first place – which may make it impossible for you to know whether it had been obtained fairly and lawfully.

There are also problems in enforcing data users to comply with the law. Personal data should not be kept longer than necessary, but how long is this? Data elements can be transferred from list to list, so a new list may consist of some elements originally collected long ago. If you overspend your credit card limit as a student, how long will this affect your credit rating? Will this black mark dog you wherever and whenever you need credit for the rest of your life? In fact this is unlikely to happen as commercial motives and ethical considerations will require data managers to use clean, up-to-date data. The worries still remain however, and we have yet to find satisfactory answers to these tricky questions.

Looking on the bright side however, database power can also be used for wholly good and benevolent ways. For instance, databases can do for community health care what they are now doing for marketing. They can be used to focus the energy of healthcare teams on those individuals in the community who need it most, and at the same time remove a huge administrative burden, making the team more effective and efficient.

A modern general practice may have six to eight doctors serving 15,000 to 25,000 patients. Patient records are still held in the old brown medical record envelope (MRE) in some practices, but they are beginning to be replaced by computer records. Old practices often employed more receptionists than doctors, and the office where they maintained the MRE filing system was often bigger than the patients' waiting room.

The wider use of databases in community health care will allow preventive care to be focused more effectvely on those specially at risk of suffering from certain diseases. We know for instance, that some people are more at risk of suffering from coronary heart disease. Men are affected more than women, overweight people more than those of correct weight, people with high blood pressure and cholesterol levels more than those with low values, people who smoke more than those who don't, and people from families where the disease has struck before more than those from families where it hasn't.

By using the same database search techniques used by the direct mailing organizations, doctors and nurses can target those of their patients who are specially at risk, and through counselling and advice, reduce the incidence of heart disease in the community. As well as avoiding much human suffering, this preventive approach should help to reduce the number of hospital cases and the costs to the NHS of treating the disease.

Computer crime

Computer networks are enmeshing the world in ever more complex patterns. This complexity is opening up opportunities for knowledge-able users to manipulate the systems illegally. If you are to stand a chance of detecting illegal use, you need to know in broad terms how it is done.

Society has been very slow in catching up with computer crime, and until very recently the courts could only use the traditional crime classifications to deal with it. But theft is difficult to prove if stolen copies cannot be found and the original data is intact. And trespass is no good for dealing with unauthorized access to a computer system. And so until 1990 prosecutors had to use theft of the small amount of electricity used during the unauthorized access as the basis for prosecution. Now however, the law has changed. The Computer Misuse Act of 1990 makes unauthorized access – or 'hacking' – illegal.

Big money is involved. The amounts lost due to computer crime are estimated at over $1 billion in the USA, and run to hundreds of millions of pounds in the UK, though we will probably never know the true extent because organizations are reluctant even to admit that they have fallen victim, for fear of losing the confidence of their customers.

Unauthorized access

There are three main ways of gaining unauthorized access:

- Wire-tapping methods
- Trial and error methods
- Password stealing

Wire tapping methods

Remote access to a central computer often involves the use of ordinary telephone lines. One way of getting hold of the password of a legitimate user is to tap into the telephone wires, perhaps in the same building before the wires go out under the street.

Masquerading

When a user phones up the central computer but before the user logs on, our hacker will switch the line to his own PC where he has written a little program to present a counterfeit screen display inviting the user to enter his or her password. The PC will record the password and then send a simulated error message and break the connection. The unsuspecting user will try again, log on successfully this time, and not think twice about the minor irregularity experienced during the logging on.

Later the hacker can log on using the legitimate user's password saved in his PC.

Piggybacking

In this method our hacker's PC is introduced into the line so that the communications from the legitimate user pass through it before being passed on to the central computer. While the legitimate user is logged on, messages can be intercepted and modified. For instance files sent from one bank to another could be intercepted and additional credits added to the hacker's account.

Trial and error methods

Search-and-try programs

Hackers often write simple programs to help them log on to remote computers. A program can be written to automate the logging on procedure, trying a different password each time. With an auto-dial modem and a search-and-try program a hacker can leave the program running all night and look in the morning to see if any attempts have been successful.

Psychological clues

Hugo Cornwall, author of *The New Hacker's Handbook*, gives a list of passwords that crop up time and time again. They include HELP TEST SYSTEM LOVE SEX REMOTE PHONE and FRED.

People usually choose passwords they will find easy to remember, so if you know something about the user, you can often guess a likely password. For instance, have you ever chosen for a password your date of birth, or the name of your spouse or children or the football team you support perhaps? If so, with a little bit of research a determined hacker could very quickly discover these and try them out.

Password stealing

Overlooking

When you enter your password, the characters are not usually echoed on the screen. That would make it too easy; the password would stay on the screen long enough for any passer-by to read. Instead the screen remains blank, but that won't stop a hacker looking over your shoulder and watching which keys you press, especially if you are a one-fingered hunt-and-peck typist.

Scavenging

Some hackers will even go to the trouble of going through the piles of rubbish thrown out by the computer department, looking for discarded code on print-outs, system documentation, memos and reports – anything that may be helpful in narrowing the search, such as a particular length or format recommended for the password.

Tampering with data

There are three distinct groups of individuals who may try to get at the data in your system to steal or damage it.

One group, hackers, do it for fun and kudos; the intellectual challenge and accolade from fellow hackers is the only motivation. Hackers often belong to international networks in contact through dial-up computerized bulletin boards which operate like the computer conferences offered by the big network service operators. Hackers' bulletin boards though are often set up as a hobby by an individual with a PC and a modem. The culture can be quite subversive – like in the early days of citizen's band radio – with hackers exchanging dial-up numbers of big systems, passwords and information on how to break in. The manager of a bulletin board is call 'sysop', for obvious reasons.

Another group of potential troublemakers are dissatisfied employees or ex-employees who may break into the central computer for revenge, or to restore a loss they believe they have unfairly suffered. Often they have inside information which makes it easier for them to get in. They may have worked in the computer department, or have knowledge of passwords, and their motivation may be theft or vandalism.

The third group are just plain criminals who happen to know something about computers. They are motivated by personal gain, and may use any of the traditional methods: fraud, illegal transfer of funds, forgery, ransom demands, espionage, blackmail... The computer versions of these crimes have produced a colourful vocabulary of popular terms.

The salami method

When an accounting system calculates employees paycheques, it does so only to the nearest penny: any small fractions of a penny are simply cut off and not paid. The salami method involves writing and inserting a few lines of code to collect all these tiny slices and transfer them to a separate account. The slices are too small for most businesses to notice, but can quickly add up to a considerable amount.

If the organization makes payments through the Banks Automated Clearing System (BACS) the payments could be made automatically to a bank account in a false name by electronic transfer of funds, and then the funds could be withdrawn from any of the bank's hole-in-the-wall machines. The irregular lines of code may never be discovered but even if they are, there can be no fingerprints to link them to any particular individual. Thus for the perpetrator the risks of being caught are very small.

Time bombs and logic bombs

Again, these are irregular lines of code inserted into a legitimate program, which will be activated automatically at a particular date, or when certain conditions are met. Computer criminals can use them in several different ways.

A computer criminal could insert a logic bomb into the central computer of an organization, which would cause the whole system to 'crash', that is, fail in a comprehensive manner, losing data and corrupting programs so that all the system software would have to be set up and reloaded to get the system running again.

Alternatively the logic bomb could be designed to display a ransom demand and then cause the program to 'hang', that is, lock up and not respond to any inputs until a particular password is entered to unlock the system again.

Legitimate software writers have been reported to be using logic bombs to make sure they get paid for the work they were contracted to do – but in more subtle ways than crudely demanding payment. The software may be coded to start malfunctioning in a less extreme manner, giving the software writer an opportunity to ask for payment of amounts owing before agreeing to correct the malfunction. This is illegal of course, but if software writers warn clients in the small print of the contract, they may still be within the law, though at present the legal position is unclear.

The Trojan horse

In Greek mythology, the well-defended city of Troy was invaded by deceiving the Trojans into thinking that a large wooden horse left outside the city walls was a gift from the gods. They pulled the horse inside the city and during the night soldiers climbed out and opened the gates. Thus any apparently innocent computer program could contain some extra mischievous lines of code and could be used as a Trojan horse. For instance, you may be tempted to load a computer game on your computer at work. If so, don't. It may not be all that it seems.

Data diddling

This is the simplest form of computer crime. It simply involves changing data or entering incorrect data. Examples might be a student hacking into the college computer system and changing the record of his or her grading or an employee gaining access to the payroll system and giving himself or herself a pay rise. Data diddling is the most common form of computer crime.

Viruses

Just as a program can be written to copy a file from disk into memory for instance, so a program can just as easily be written to copy itself into a free area of memory. Then the two copies will copy themselves to give four copies. The four will become eight, then sixteen. . . . Very soon the whole memory will be filled with copies of a program which has no purpose other than to reproduce itself. At this point the computer will stop, completely disabled.

Any program that can replicate itself automatically is called a virus. They can be attached to seemingly innocent programs which act as Trojan horses to carry the virus, or they can contain instructions which allow the virus to be spread through a computer network. Thus they are very infectious and extremely dangerous.

In 1988 a student at Cornell University unleashed a virus into the InterNet/Arpanet computer network which connects university and Department of Defense research laboratories across the USA. It did damage which cost close on $1 billion to put right, and the student, Robert Morris, was found guilty and sentenced to four hundred hours of community service and a fine of $10,000 dollars.

Computer security

There can never be a 100 per cent secure system. If enough people are determined to break in, sooner or later someone will find a way. Part of the problem is that the more secure you make a system, the less easy it is for bona fide users to use. There has to be a compromise, and the costs of the inevitable breaches must be budgeted for. For instance a couple of years ago, Visa International, the credit card organization, budgeted for a loss of more than £130m in fraud. However, they said that was acceptable because it represented less than 1 per cent of turnover.

Computer security depends on a combination of physical barriers, software defences and security procedures.

Physical barriers consist of making sure that computers and terminals are locked up and only accessible to legitimate users. It is also important to make sure that disks and tapes are similarly protected.

Networks make physical barriers difficult, because telephone wires cannot be completely protected physically. However, for extremely sensitive telecommunications links, such as those connecting military computers to missile launching facilities, physical barriers are used. The cable is passed down a pipe containing a pressurized gas. If any attempt is made to break into the pipe, the pressure drop will be detected and trigger an alarm.

Software defences usually depend on passwords, personal identification numbers (PINs) in conjunction with cards, and cryptography. Passwords should be changed regularly. If you are ever responsible for systems security, make sure users choose passwords which are not proper names or real words, preferably a random mixture of letters in upper and lower case, numbers and punctuation marks, to make it difficult for hackers to guess. The danger then of course is that legitimate users will forget their numbers, or worse still, write them down in accessible places. Often a satisfactory compromise is to choose an easily remembered word or number, with one or two random characters introduced somewhere in the middle.

Cards and PINs similar to those used with credit cards can also be used, and cryptography can also be employed to code transmissions across networks in such a way that only the intended user can decode the message.

And finally, procedures should be in place to ensure that codes and passwords are changed regularly, and that audits of system performance are regularly carried out. The system should maintain files of all transactions, so that an audit trail can be followed by an auditor to check that no irregular transactions have occurred.

Trends: managing information in the future

There are four trends which we can identify and use to anticipate how managing information in the future may develop:

- Advances in technology
- Cheaper computers
- More costly humans
- Continuing change

Advances in technology

An argument for putting off buying a new computer is to save on the cost of the purchase. Why? Because the price of a given level of performance drops by about half every two years. This has been true over the last thirty years, and shows every sign of continuing to be true into the future.

It certainly makes it expensive to stay at the leading edge of developments, but if you are prepared to purchase hardware based on two-year-old technology, you can turn the argument around and save money by buying a computer now.

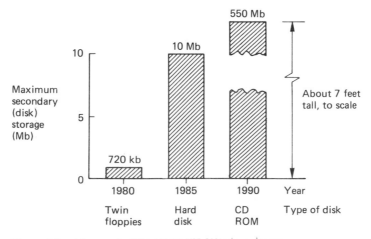

Figure 6.2 Advances in PC memory and secondary storage

One measure of performance is the amount of storage available in a computer. Take a look at the way main memory and secondary storage in the PC has increased over the years (Figure 6.2).

Main memory, you will remember, is the actual computer circuits which hold the software you are using and the files you are working on, so with more main memory you can run more sophisticated programs, and you can process larger files. Secondary storage is any kind of permanent storage. Tape is used for batch processing and archiving, but is no good for on-line, interactive processing which is the trend now. Disks are required for that, so the computer can go straight to a particular file anywhere on the disk, instead of having to start at the beginning and 'fast forward' through all the earlier files.

Another performance measure is the speed with which a computer carries out the fundamental instructions that are the elementary bricks from which all programs are built. These are measured in MIPS, millions of instructions per second, and the speed continues to grow. You notice the difference immediately if you go back to using an old word processor after using a new one: the time it takes to scroll through a long document soon gets your fingers drumming.

Computer peripheral hardware such as printers, secondary storage and screens are all still developing.

- Printers have passed through dot matrix and daisy wheel to laser and ink jet in the space of twenty years. Prior to that the old teletypewriter had reigned supreme for decades.
- Secondary storage in the 1960s consisted of stacks of punched cards and punched paper tapes. These soon gave way to magnetic tape and Winchester disks, then floppy disks: originally 8 inch diameter, then 5.25 inch and now 3.5 inch. It seems unlikely that magnetic media will be developed much further, but the CD-ROM, Compact Disk Read-only Memory, and solid state devices will probably be developed further.
- Screens have only recently been developed beyond the TV technology of the 1960s. Development was stimulated by the arrival of the lap-top PC in the mid 1980s which required a flat screen. Then in less than ten years screens advanced from tiny LCD, liquid crystal displays in black and grey, through black and orange plasma discharge displays, to full size, full colour flat screens based on the TFT, Thin Film Transistor technology to be launched by IBM and Toshiba soon, probably in 1993.

Cheaper computers

In 1951 the Univac computer cost $2.5 million. By 1980 it could be duplicated on a single circuit board costing less than $500.

In 1976 one megabyte of RAM main memory cost $170,000. By 1979, three years later it had fallen to $15,000. Now it costs about $80.

In 1960 one megabyte of disk space cost $130. Now it costs less than $1.

On average, over thirty years, the cost of a given level of computing power has fallen by about half every two years.

More costly humans

People on the other hand are becoming more expensive to employ. Standards of living continue to rise, and so too do people's expectations. Someone earning £2,000 per annum in 1970 would expect at least £25,000 in 1992 for the same job. As a result, services are tending to get more expensive in real terms, at a time when many manufactured goods, especially computers, have fallen in price.

Continuing change

Everything seems to indicate that we are in for a period of change which will continue at least for some years to come.

- Throughout the world, political change is sweeping away nationalized industries and reducing state regulation.
- By the end of 1992, the UK should be fully integrated into the European Community. The last quotas, tariffs and other barriers to free trade throughout Europe should be removed.
- Eastern Europe, Russia and the CIS will develop as huge new markets and opportunities for investment.
- Organizations will be exposed to competition of growing intensity, as markets become increasingly globalized.
- Buyers' markets are likely to prevail as more and more sectors of world markets become oversupplied. The consumer is firmly in the driving seat, and is unlikely to give it up. Services and products will sell on quality, delivery, variety and price.

Only a major catastrophe of world-wide proportions could halt these trends. Of course it is possible that a political crisis may lead to:

another world war, or
a breakdown in international trade, or
a world-wide economic depression

– but so long as we can avoid global disasters, the trends seem set to continue.

So what are the implications? What should you and your organization do, and what plans should you make to take advantage of these trends? Read them through again, and see if you agree with them.

They all point to more intense competition, which will require organizations to:

● Use human resources efficiently, and
● use human resources effectively.

Using human resources efficiently means using them as little as possible for tasks that can be automated. It is efficient to use one person and a JCB digger to shift earth instead of twenty people with picks and shovels. Similarly we must find ways to automate the handling of all our routine information. Information systems are cheaper, faster and less prone to errors.

Using human resources effectively means using them for the tasks they are good at, and for which computers are quite useless. We need people, not computers, for the creative, imaginative, inquisitive roles that are essential in good design, research and development. We should use people to make value judgements, to develop their inspirational and intuitive abilities to forecast trends and tune in to customer needs. And above all we need people to push forward, to motivate, to switch on the computers and keep them running, and to carry the organization forward towards its goals.

For you as a manager somewhere in the middle of your organization, this may sound great in theory; you may agree with these conclusions, but what can you actually do? The way you manage your information is dependent on the total system in which you work. How open are channels of communication? If your organization is bureaucratic or needs a new management information system there is little you can do about that, apart from lobbying for change, and being ready to play a role when opportunities arise.

The effective and efficient use of humans at work is intimately connected with the way information is managed throughout the organization. This partly depends on computer skills, and knowledge of techniques like the kaizen tools which you can use, but to a much greater extent it depends on more general management developments such as the move towards flatter organizational structures, Japanese management styles, intrapreneuring, empowerment and Total Quality Management. The responsibility for initiating these developments lies at the top of the organization.

Teams throughout the organization must be empowered and motivated to make decisions, and this means, in the words of George Fisher, Chief Executive of Motorola headquarters in Chicago, 'The notion of control has to be thrown in question.' He accepts that he cannot directly control more than an insignificant part of Motorola's world-wide operations. His influence however lies in his power to strongly encourage a culture of staying close to the customer, and empowering individuals and teams to make their own decisions.

Technology has a big potential role to play in aiding human interaction within and between teams. The new jargon terms are groupware and CSCW, which stands for Computer Supported Cooperative Work. In 1990 Japan's Ministry of International Trade and Industry launched an eight-year project aimed at developing CSCW. The Japanese have already shown us how to use teams to cut waste and eliminate quality problems. And that was without using groupware. By 1998 will we be left sitting at our solitary PCs while the Japanese use CSCW to work in large international teams researching and developing their way to even greater dominance in world markets?

To meet the continually rising expectations of our customer, the global citizen, we must learn how best to manage information, which is, in the words of John Sculley, Chief Executive at Apple Computers, the strategic resource of the 1990s.

Competence self-assessment

1   What is the name of the act of parliament recently passed to deal with computer crime? Why was the existing criminal law unsatisfactory for dealing with computer crime?

2   Describe in three or four lines for each, the salami method, the Trojan horse and the logic bomb.

3   To what kind of attack from a computer criminal do you think your system at work may be most vulnerable? What defences should be introduced to guard against possible attack? Should you change any of your own practices?

4   List some changes in your organization's use of information technology over the last five years. What changes do you anticipate will occur at work in the next five years? What should you personally do in preparation?

5   What does CSCW stand for, and how can it be implemented? What two prerequisites are necessary for success?

References and further reading

Cornwall, H. (1986). *The New Hacker's Handbook*. Century Hutchinson.
Dizard, Jr, W. P. (1982). *The Coming Information Age. An Overview of Technology, Economics, and Politics* (2nd edn). Longman.

Glossary

ABC analysis – see Pareto analysis.

Alphanumeric characters – all the upper and lower case letters of the alphabet, and the numbers 0 to 9.

ANSI – American National Standards Institute. The American equivalent of the British Standards Institute.

ASCII – American Standard Code for Information Interchange. A set of codes which uses eight bits for each alphanumeric character, plus a range of punctuation marks and simple graphics characters. Originally used for teletypewriters and punched paper tape storage of keystrokes, and now widely used for computer communications.

BIM – British Institute of Management, the previous name of the Institute of Management.

Binary code – a coding system which uses binary numbers to represent alphabetical letters and decimal numbers.

Binary numbers – a number system like the decimal system, but instead of using ten digits it only uses two: 0 and 1.

Bit – contraction of the term 'binary digit'. It means a single element or figure in binary code – a 0 or a 1.

BOM – bill of materials. A structured parts-list for a finished assembly. The BOM has the finished assembly at level 0, the main sub-assemblies at level 1, the parts required for the sub-assemblies at level 2, the materials required for the parts at level 3, etc. The BOM therefore contains information not only about what materials and parts go into the product, but also information about the order in which the parts are put together during manufacture.

Byte – a set of eight bits. This is the practical minimum number of bits handled by a computer at any one time. In ASCII, one byte is required to represent each of the alphanumeric characters.

CAD – computer-aided design. Special software which allows a computer to be used for preparing designs and drawings. New designs can sometimes be produced very quickly by calling up a previous similar design onto the screen and 'editing' it.

CAM – computer-aided manufacture. A catch-all term to describe any production machinery which runs under computer control.

CIM – computer-integrated manufacture. a comprehensive network of computers and CNC machines which allows a factory to be controlled digitally, without the use of production paperwork, from design all the way through production to delivery.

CNC – computer numerical control. A system of programs and hardware used to control the tool paths, speeds and feed rates of production machinery used for cutting and forming parts made usually of metal.

CSCW – computer supported co-operative work. A generic term to cover the team use of teleconferencing, e-mail and any other 'groupware'.

Digital – literally means data which is held in the form of a series of numbers, but usually it is used to imply binary coded data held in electronic or magnetic form.

EDI – electronic data interchange. The exchange of commercial information between customer and supplier in digital form, directly between their respective computers, or via an intermediate third party computer service.

E-mail – electronic mail, sent through a network from one computer screen to one or many other screens. Almost instantaneous communication, far quicker than snail-mail, the old postal system.

Gantt chart – a horizontal bar chart, with calendar dates across the top, advancing to the right. Down the left side is a list of orders, or people, or machines or activities. Thus bars can be drawn in to represent periods of time when orders are being worked on, persons are on holiday, machines are occupied or activities are being performed. The length of a bar represents its duration and the ends show its start and finish dates.

Groupware – software to encourage cooperation between the members of a group. It usually offers members a common view of the data being worked upon, and depends on communications and database facilities.

Histogram – a diagram in which columns or vertical bars side by side and touching, are used to represent frequencies of various ranges of values of a quantity.

Intrapreneuring – the encouragement of an entrepreneuring spirit amongst managers and employees. Progress through the taking of small risks is encouraged and rewarded.

Inventory – another name for stocks of materials, WIP and finished goods.

ISDN – integrated systems digital network. This is a communications standard for new networks being set up by British Telecom and Mercury to handle high-speed, real-time digital communication. These networks can also carry voice and moving video, and so are ideally suited for teleconferencing.

Ishikawa diagram – a fishbone diagram for analysing the root causes of some observed effect. Invented by Kaouru Ishikawa, the Japanese professor.

IT – information technology. This term covers all the hardware and software used for storing, processing or communicating information. It includes computers, telephones, satellites, fibre optics, videos, etc.

JIT – just in time. A system of production where products are transferred from process to process in transfer batches of one, with almost no buffer stocks between processes. When a process somewhere in the middle of the production routing finishes its processing and passes an item to the next process downstream, it should receive another item from the process upstream 'just in time' to keep it busy. The system depends on tight scheduling, and the highest levels of manufacturing quality.

Kaizen – the Japanese word for continual improvement.

LAN – local area network. A term used to describe the network of communications links connecting up the computers on a single site.

LCD – liquid crystal display. The type of display used for digital watches, with black characters against a greenish grey background, sometimes backlit. Large LCD displays are commonly used for portable computer screens.

Lead-time – the time that elapses between ordering the manufacture or delivery of something, and subsequently receiving it.

Lorenz curve – this is another name for the Pareto curve. See Pareto analysis.

MIS – management information system. A network of computers linked up to a central large computer and database, used for accessing, storing, processing and communicating management information within an organization.

Modem – a contraction of the term 'modulator-demodulator'. It is a piece of gear which translates computer binary signals into sounds for transmitting through the telephone network. When the sounds arrive, the modem at the other end converts the sounds back into binary code which the receiving computer can understand.

MPS – master production schedule. A statement of the total requirements of finished products to be produced week by week for the next six months or so. It is the final result which the production planning department should be aiming to achieve, and is derived from sales forecasts and orders received.

MRP – materials requirement planning. Computer software for working out when parts should be made, and when materials should be ordered. It takes the master production schedule which is a statement of the weekly requirements of finished goods, and then works backwards in time to find out when the parts and raw materials should be scheduled to be delivered.

MRP-2 – manufacturing resource planning. MRP software which has been developed and enhanced to take in the scheduling of all manufacturing resources for a given MPS, not just materials and parts, but also the acquisition of finance, machinery, personnel, etc.

Normal curve – a symmetrical bell-shaped curve, which often crops up when the histogram is plotted for a set of figures which tend to cluster around a central or average value.

Parallel communications – a system of communications in which the eight bits of a byte travel in parallel down eight parallel wires to arrive simultaneously at their destination. Thus it is eight times as fast as an equivalent serial link.

Pareto analysis – also known as ABC analysis and 80/20 analysis. It is used to sort out the important few items from amongst the less important many other items, and is named after Vilfredo Pareto, an Italian economist who discovered that 20 per cent of the population of a country will typically own 80 per cent of the wealth of that country. The analysis is performed by ranking the individuals in order of descending wealth, then finding the worth of the first 20 per cent.

PERT – project evaluation and review technique. This is a project planning and control method which involves representing all the various component activities as arrows arranged in their logical order. Some activities can be carried out in parallel, and some activities cannot start until other activities have been completed and so must be chained in sequence. The result is a network, and the longest chain – or critical path – through the network determines the minimum time required for completion of the whole project. The underlying method is also known as critical path analysis.

Quality circles – a group of workers who meet outside normal working hours to discuss ways of improving the way things are done at work. The groups, also known as quality improvement teams, are paid for their extra efforts and encouraged by management to study and acquire any skills they may need. These groups of up to ten workers are often led by a supervisor, who acts as coach, mentor and adviser.

R-chart – a continuous graph of the range of values found in samples of fixed size taken from the output of a process. If the ranges charted begin to grow, an upward trend will begin to show, indicating that variability is on the increase. This may not affect the average size being produced if the variation causes values to occur both further above and below the average. Without the R-chart an increase in variation may thus go undetected.

RAM – random access memory. In theory this means memory where an item of stored data can be accessed without the need to read through all earlier items to find it, as is the case with serial access media such as magnetic tape. In practice, RAM is now only used to describe the memory circuits of a computer which hold data and programs while the computer is switched on. Each item of data has its own address in memory and can be accessed directly.

Revenue – the total income of an organization before any costs are deducted.

ROM – read-only memory. A form of computer memory which cannot be erased or changed, and which is not lost when the computer is switched off or re-set. It is used for instance to hold the small set of coded instructions telling the computer where to look for the operating system when it is first switched on or re-set.

Run chart – a continuous graph for monitoring single samples taken from the output of a process. If there is any drift or gradual change taking place, it will show up as a trend on the graph.

Serial communications – a communications system in which the eight bits of a byte travel in series, one after the other down a single wire. It is a simple system which can use telephone wires for long-distance communications.

Spreadsheet – a computer program which divides the screen up into columns and rows. At the intersection of each column and row is a cell which can contain a value or a formula which the computer will compute. Thus for instance a column of figures can be entered, and the total automatically found by entering a formula at the foot of the column. It is also possible to sort figures into order, present the figures in the form of a graph etc.

Standard deviation – a measure of scatter, or variability in a set of figures. The simplest measure of scatter is the range – calculated by subtracting the smallest value from the largest value – but this is unreliable because it is derived from just two figures. The standard deviation however is derived from every figure in the set. The first step in its calculation is to find the deviation, or distance of every figure from the average for the set.

Teleconferencing – users on a network, accessing a central database and communicating with each other in real-time by text messages, and sometimes also by voice and video pictures. The users share a joint view of their work, which may be in the form of text, graphics, scanned images and hand drawings.

Teleworking – using a phone, fax and computer communications to work from home instead of commuting to work every day.

TQM – total quality management. A management philosophy which trains, encourages and empowers everyone in the organization to apply a systematic approach to manage their own work and solve their own problems. Whoever receives the output of your work becomes your 'customer', and exceeding his or her needs should be paramount.

VANs – value added network services. A term used to describe a network provider who does more than just carry messages. Examples are providers of e-mail facilities, and EDI services for instance.

Voice-mail – a system for storing voice messages for retrieval by the addressee(s). It works in much the same way as e-mail, and the messages may be stored digitally and reconstituted only when the addressee logs on to collect mail.

WAN – wide area network. The network of communications links used to connect up computers which are located on several different sites, sometimes on different continents.

WIP – work in progress, or work in process. It consists of partly completed work: sub-assemblies for building into finished goods, partly machined products, etc.

X-bar chart – a continuous graph of the average values of small samples of fixed size taken from the output of a process. It is at least twenty times more sensitive than the run-chart in detecting small changes in the output.

Index